Inspirational Coffee Breaks

for Women

12 Ground Rules for Pouring Your Heart into Life!

To Sarah,

Julie Clark

With Warmth,

ISBN: 978-0-9828683-0-0

Cover design by Kim Casault of Cruxwire Web

For additional copies of this book, contact:

The Inspirational Coffee Club
Julie Clark, Founder
PO Box 87922
Sioux Falls, South Dakota 57109
Email: Julie@theinspirationalcoffeeclub.com
Website: www.theinspirationalcoffeeclub.com

Printed in the United States of America

First Edition

This book is dedicated:

To Mom
Who's my all-time favorite coffee break companion.

To Dad
Who's shown me that a cracked cup can indeed be a treasure.

To Brad
Who (for a non-coffee drinker) is pretty darned wonderful.

To the members of my personal Coffee Club
Who without your encouragement, support, and sometimes gentle 'kick in the cup,' this book would not be possible.

To Grandma
My very first coffee break companion. I can only imagine how amazing coffee breaks are in Heaven!

I love you all very much!

Contents

Welcome to Inspirational Coffee Breaks!

Warmest Greetings,

Believe it or not, I've been taking coffee breaks since I was three-years old. My very first coffee break companion was my Grandma. To this day, I treasure the time I spent with Grandma because she showed me just how special coffee breaks could be. My favorite memories together are the times we spent baking sugar cookies, and while we waited for them to cool, Grandma would put on a fresh pot of coffee. I remember how grown-up I felt as she'd push my chair snugly up to the kitchen table, pour me my very own cup of coffee, and hand me a cookie to go along with our 'coffee break.' Grandma taught me a special technique— dunking my sugar cookies into my coffee. I knew back then I had discovered something wonderful, and I've carried that love of coffee breaks into adulthood.

I've never forgotten the day when I was helping my Grandma prepare for one of her monthly Coffee Club gatherings, and a friend of hers saw me dunking cookies into my coffee. She shouted to my Grandma, *"Delores, you can't let Julie drink coffee. It will stunt her growth!"* I am so glad my Grandma didn't listen to that friend because coffee has done anything but stunt my growth. In fact, over the years, I have found coffee to be a powerful teacher for life.

From my early years of enjoying treasured coffee breaks with my Grandma to the current days of sharing cherished coffee time with my mom and my friends, coffee has played a critical role in my development through the years. In my coffee, I have discovered valuable life lessons for living life to the fullest—what I call the *12 Ground Rules for Life.* These are key strategies that I embrace and am passing along to you through an innovative approach to personal fulfillment I've termed *Inspirational Coffee Breaks.* It's one that I am excited to share with you and hope will become a life-changing practice for you as well.

Inspirational Coffee Breaks for Women has the potential to turn your regular coffee breaks into something distinctive and memorable. My hope is that it will give you a fresh boost of encouragement, hope, and wisdom for life. This book is designed to take you on a personal journey to reconnect with the wonderful woman you are, offering creative techniques for reinvigorating your soul and awakening your best life. As you've probably realized, creating a life brimming with happiness and fulfillment doesn't just happen. It has to be worked at. There's a wonderful life waiting for you, but it's up to you to brew it. The *12 Ground Rules* contained in this book are meant to be a treasured recipe for life, filling your heart and soul with uplifting strategies to help you pour your heart back into *your* life! When implemented regularly, they will help you create a life that overflows with the kind of enjoyment you so richly deserve.

I hope you find a quiet, comfortable spot—whether it's in your favorite coffee shop or curled up at home in a comfy chair. Grab your favorite beverage (that's right—I don't discriminate against you non-coffee drinkers!) and treat yourself to the power of these *Inspirational Coffee Breaks*. You will brew up many personal insights into who you are and how you want to live the rest of your life. Each chapter is overflowing with refreshing, thought-provoking questions and easy-to-apply action steps you can blend into your daily life. Whether you are a coffee drinker or not, the principles in this book will certainly be ones you can relate to. I recommend having a journal and pen nearby because you'll want to take notes.

If you let them, *Inspirational Coffee Breaks* can be the start of a freshly-brewed future. They can provide the lifting power necessary to help you cherish where you've been while savoring all the possibilities still in front of you. I commend you for taking hold of a process that will help your life take on new meaning and fulfillment. I tip my cup to you and the beginning of many *Inspirational Coffee Breaks*. May your cup overflow with happiness, success, and joy!

Julie

Julie Clark, Founder
The Inspirational Coffee Club

Want an Extra Jolt of Inspiration?

There is a huge difference between reading these *12 Ground Rules* and actually implementing and living them. The more you study these *Ground Rules*, the more natural they become. And, the more you live them out in your daily life, the more fulfilled you will become. To get the most enjoyment and benefit out of this book, I encourage you to gather your own personal Coffee Club to share this invigorating journey. Get around other women and enjoy *Inspirational Coffee Breaks* together!

Every woman wants to live her best life. Your very own Inspirational Coffee Club can give you the support to make that happen. It's the perfect blend of fun, rejuvenation, and motivation. Sometimes we all need a little encouraging, nurturing, accountability, and a good 'kick in the cup' to get us moving. When we come together with other women, we strengthen ourselves because we know we are not alone. When we are supported by others, we are empowered to make the changes we may not make on our own. Imagine what a difference your own Inspirational Coffee Club will make on your life!

Use the Grounds for Thoughts questions in each chapter as discussion topics to learn, share, discuss, and connect with each other. Challenge and support one another to take the Grounds for Actions steps to apply each principle to your daily life. Ideally, I think it's best to cover one Ground Rule a month, but some of you may want to meet more often, and that's just fine. It's up to you. After all, it's your Coffee Club! You'll be surprised at how a little bit of added accountability and encouragement will change your life. Your own Coffee Club will help you move deeper into these concepts—into what you are experiencing and feeling and help you learn even more about yourself.

You may want to try out different coffee shops in your area or take turns hosting coffee breaks in your homes, offices, churches, and so forth. When you meet for coffee and actively practice these Ground Rules, somewhere in the midst of all the sipping and chatting, *Inspirational Coffee Breaks* work their magic. They will refresh you, invigorate you, and make you want to breathe in the delicious aroma of life. Your own Inspirational Coffee Club truly is like a double shot of espresso for life. Visit www.theinspirationalcoffeeclub.com for information on organizing your own Coffee Club.

GROUND RULE #1

Schedule Inspirational Coffee Breaks ~ Refill Your Mind, Body, and Soul

"You are the most important asset you have; treat yourself accordingly."
Lucy MacDonald

Breaks At This Job of Life Are Not Optional— They're Required!

"The name of the game is taking care of yourself, because you're going to live long enough to wish you had." Grace Mirabella

If you are like most women, you probably pour yourself endlessly out to others. You go the extra mile for your children, spouse, parents, career, friends, church, and community to put other people's needs first. In fact, that's part of what makes you so special. Managing careers, families, and volunteer activities can be fun, but it can also be draining. Our routines weigh us down and before you know it, you're exhausted, tired, and just plain burned out. When you are exhausted at the end of the day, you simply do not have energy to spend on yourself. But if you continue to pour yourself out to others without ever filling yourself back up, you'll soon be going through life on empty. The truth is you cannot be your best self when you are constantly running on empty.

The world is filled with so many women walking around emptied— overwhelmed, burned out, depressed, stressed, exhausted, and out of touch with themselves. Maybe you are one of them. Many of us have no idea how burned out we really are. We keep ourselves so busy that we don't even realize we've stopped taking care of ourselves. In fact, research shows that 80% (that's 4 out of 5 women) are burned out. So many of us are trying to do everything. We believe we don't have time to take care of ourselves. If you're one of those who is always going and always doing, you need to stop and learn how to refill yourself before you run dry. Things around you will start to falter if you continue to run on empty.

I'm going to let you in on a little secret: how busy you are has nothing to do with how fully you are living life. Today most women are juggling more than ever but sadly, most of us are less happy and less fulfilled than ever before. What good does it do to get so much done if we're emptying ourselves in the process? Fulfillment does not come from doing more. In fact, emptiness comes when we try to do too much. Constant activity dulls us from living our best life. Consider the story of the two woodcutters.

 **Second Cup Story:**

Once upon a time two very strong woodcutters got a job chopping down trees. The boss gave them both an axe and told them that the man who chopped the most wood by the end of the day would be handsomely rewarded. The one man worked non-stop the entire day, chopping madly to get as much done as possible. The other man, however, took time to stop for short, regular breaks every few hours.

At the end of the day, the boss came to see who had chopped the most wood. Obviously, the man who had worked all day without any breaks knew he had to have cut the most wood because he never took a rest. Ironically, it was the man who took the short, frequent breaks who actually chopped more wood.

The woodcutter asked in shock, *"How could that be? I never took a break while you stopped every few hours!"*

To which the other replied, *"Yes, but if you'd noticed, each time I stopped to break, I was taking time to sharpen my axe."*

Most of us are like that first woodcutter—we get so caught up in this mentality of 'being productive' that we often sacrifice ourselves. Usually, when the activity of daily life attempts to drain us, the first thing we eliminate is the very thing we need most—a quiet break from the daily grind to refill ourselves. Time to relax, regroup, and renew. Time to 'sharpen' ourselves for what lies ahead. Instead, we just keep pushing forward, refusing to lose pace, determined to do everything. We derive pleasure from seeing how much we can cram into each day. But few of us realize how this busy lifestyle robs us of the physical and mental energy we need to be our best selves. Many people are not only destroying their physical bodies at this pace, but even more tragic, they are emptying their minds and souls as well.

Regular breaks from the daily grind are essential for a high-quality life. You need to start slowing down and reducing your pace. But restoring your body is just part of it. If you renew your body, but spend no time on your mind and soul, you'll continue to feel empty. Rest for your body is necessary, but invigoration for your soul is what truly makes your life come alive again. It's what allows us to 'sharpen' ourselves so we can become the woman we are truly meant to be. Inspirational Coffee Breaks are a perfect blend of relaxation for your tired body and invigoration for your mind and soul. (And you don't have to be a coffee drinker to enjoy them!) It's the opportunity to refill that part of you that has been emptied and dulled by life and all its responsibilities. It's time to shift the focus back on taking care of you for a change.

A recent survey from the Massachusetts Institute of Technology (MIT) strongly suggests that coffee breaks—or at least breaks from activity—actually increase a person's productivity. Just as a coffee break gives people a chance to wind down slightly and re-group for the remaining work of the day, an Inspirational Coffee Break is a chance to relax and re-group for the remainder of your life and your responsibilities that lie ahead. Your efficiency and productivity actually go down when you try to do too much. Even if you have a to-do list a mile long, take a short break, and you'll be more productive when you come back to reality. Just 15-30 minutes can be enough to rejuvenate you.

We *all* need to take time to pause every day so that we can refill ourselves to effectively meet the demands of our busy lives. A daily Inspirational Coffee Break practice will change your life. If you aren't taking time to refill your mind, body, and soul, you are leaving so much happiness on the table! Having a daily practice to refill myself is one of the single most powerful strategies I've found for living my best life.

Don't risk going through life being one of those women who takes care of everyone else before taking care of herself. You cannot live your best life when you are so out of touch with yourself. Living life more fully starts with learning to be as nurturing and respectful of yourself as you are of other people. To be a great mom, wife, daughter, employee, boss, or friend you must first be a great you. This means you need to keep your body and mind healthy. Don't neglect yourself. Women who do not properly take care of themselves now will only hurt themselves in years to come. Eventually, you are going to get so dulled and burned out that you will be no good to your family, your office, or anyone else if you are run down.

Do you want to be one of those women who goes through life full of energy or drained of it? One that's deeply connected to herself or barely knows who she is anymore? When you begin making Inspirational Coffee Breaks a part of your life, you will start to feel your*self* returning. Not only will you feel more energized physically, but you'll also become mentally stronger. Making the decision to take care of yourself is the ultimate first step in adding more fulfillment to your life. As I finish this section, I am snuggled up in a blanket, sitting by my cozy fireplace after a long day, sipping a freshly-brewed cup of coffee. My body and spirit just feel so full. It's time that you learned how to give yourself a little bit of 'you' time as well. To start living your best life you need to reclaim the right to take better care of yourself. A happier you starts with having a healthy mind, body, and soul. Following are suggestions for taking your own Inspirational Coffee Breaks.

Grounds for Thought: Are you taking good care of yourself or are you driving yourself like a workhorse? How much time have you taken for yourself this week? Is your life draining the spirit right out of you? Are you one of those women who are walking around empty right now?

JAVA JOLT #1:
Quit Drinking the "I Feel So Guilty Blend" On Your Breaks

"Self-care is not about self-indulgence, it's about self-preservation." Audrey Lorde

If you're one of the few lucky ones, you can take time for yourself without feeling guilty. But if you're like the rest of us, the moment you decide to take a little time out for yourself that nasty guilt creeps in and keeps us from really enjoying any downtime. Just as we start to sit down to enjoy a little break, the list of all the things we 'should' and 'ought' to be doing instead runs through our minds. We somehow feel we're lazy or we're not doing enough if we take some time for ourselves. In fact, the moment we have a little bit of free time we usually fill it with something else so we don't have to feel that guilt. Those of you who are drinking this "I Feel So Guilty Blend" during your breaks need to learn to pour it out and start drinking something fresh. Otherwise, the guilt will prevent you from truly enjoying any downtime you take for yourself.

Think taking a little time to renew yourself is selfish? Think again!

Keep going through life at the pace you currently are and you will get sick and then who will take care of you? Surely we have obligations to others but none are greater than our obligation to look after ourselves. You must take care of yourself because your life depends on it. Remember this: *only to the extent that you take care of yourself are you able to take care of others.* You can't give what you do not have. The more alert and sensitive you are to your own needs, the more loving and generous you can be to those around you. Learning to incorporate regular Inspirational Coffee Breaks into your daily life is a strong life practice that gives you the strength to care more effectively for those who rely on you.

"You take care of you for me, and I will take care of me for you." Jim Rohn

Studies show that not taking care of ourselves is unhealthy for those who depend on us. You don't do your family, friends, or work any good when you are so burned out. The best example you can give others is to take the time to care for yourself. When you neglect yourself physically, spiritually, and mentally you neglect everyone important to you. They aren't getting the best of you. If you are going around empty you have nothing left to give others. When you learn to take care of yourself, you are more engaged, energetic, and enthusiastic, therefore, helping those around you even more. Consider this example.

 **Second Cup Story:**
For those of you who have ever flown before, you're probably familiar with the flight attendant's overview on how to properly use the oxygen masks in the event of an emergency:*"Place your oxygen mask on yourself BEFORE placing it on someone else."* By doing this you can then care more effectively for others around you.

How true is that statement for life! We can't help others if we have neglected to fill ourselves up first. The honest-to-goodness truth is that you have to come first—at least some of the time. Securing your own oxygen mask is the most selfless and helpful thing you can do for everyone else. But this is too often opposite of how people live their lives. Instead, they run around helping everyone else with their oxygen masks (errands, requests, obligations, etc.) and eventually run out of oxygen themselves becoming stressed, tired, unfit, and unhealthy. Are you putting on your oxygen mask first or are you securing everyone else's before yours?

Taking time to restore yourself can help everyone around you. The best thing you can give your family and friends is a happy, fulfilled woman. When we learn to care for ourselves, we naturally begin to take care of others more effectively without resentment or frustration. When I don't take regular time for renewal I can absolutely tell. I become more easily stressed and irritable. And normally those I love most get the brunt of it. Even the good feelings that come from being available to others diminish as you start to resent all you do. Can any of you relate? Without regular time to refill your body and soul, you begin to feel exhausted, stressed, irritable, and someone other than the wonderful, loving woman you want to be. Believe it or not, you actually give both yourself and your loved ones an important gift when you start making time for yourself—your own happiness.

It takes courage to put yourself first for once because it's not something that comes naturally for most of us. Pour out that "I Feel So Guilty Blend!" Give yourself permission to make the quality of your life your top priority. After all, a high quality life begins with a high quality you. Sometimes you just need to admit that you need—and deserve—a time out from your life. When you start making Inspirational Coffee Breaks a regular priority in your life, you reconnect with the woman you want to be, and it makes you a better all-around woman—wife, daughter, mom, sister, leader, co-worker, and friend. Everyone benefits from a better you! Remember, if you take care of yourself first, you will have more to give others. Best of all, you will appreciate and enjoy those around you more than you have in a long time.

Grounds for Thought: Do you have a healthy balance of caring for your own needs along with the needs of others? Or are you so good at keeping everyone happy—your kids, your spouse, your parents, your friends, your career—that, in doing so, you've neglected to care for yourself? Do you feel guilty when you take time for yourself?

Grounds for Action: When you take time for yourself and guilt rears its ugly face, say out loud, *"I will not feel guilty for refilling myself for a change."* Grab a clean coffee filter (or a sticky note if you're not a coffee drinker), and write the words: I AM WORTH IT! Tape this somewhere you will see it daily as a constant reminder that you are worthy of some valuable time for yourself.

JAVA JOLT #2:
Schedule Your Breaks or You Won't Get Them

"The time to relax is when you don't have time for it." Sydney J. Harris

One of the main statements I hear so many women say is, *"I just don't have the time to spend on me!"* I'm going to give you a gentle reality check—you have the same twenty-four hours a day as everyone else. Do you think that women who make regular time for themselves are just less busy? Not likely. Instead, they have made their own self-restoration a priority. They've learned to take control of their daily schedule and reprioritize their lives so they can give both to themselves as well as to others. *'No time'* is just an excuse to keep yourself feeling empty and unfulfilled. If you can't make 15-30 minutes to renew yourself each day, you're choosing busyness over your life. And if you're too busy, you'll never live your best life.

So many women rush through life, telling themselves that eventually life will slow down and then they will have time to focus on themselves. But when? Do you see an opening in your schedule today? This week? This month? Realistically, the world around you is unlikely to slow down. It's up to you to create the time you need. It's not that your life gets busy—*you* get busy. Remember, you control your schedule. Your schedule should not control you. Getting your schedule under control is one of the surest ways I know to create more happiness. You need to reclaim your time and carve out some time for yourself on a regular basis (preferably daily). That means putting yourself on the schedule before anyone and anything else. You must stop letting life's schedules get away from you and start making your life more of a priority.

I've learned full well that unless you schedule time for your breaks, you most likely will never get them. Our time is limited and we are juggling so many other demands. So the plain truth is, unless you *make* time for yourself, it will never *find* you. You control your schedule. If you're serious about taking better care of yourself and commit to it, you'll schedule the time. We make time for the things that are most important to us. Let me give you some suggestions to help you make more time for yourself.

First, give yourself permission to leave some things undone while you restore yourself for awhile. So many of us have a hard time enjoying any downtime until all the work is done. This 'work' can mean anything—the last load of laundry to be done, the closet to be organized, the dishes to be done, the bills to be paid. There's this awful myth in society that says when you get everything done, you'll finally be able to relax. But if you wait until everything is done, you'll never get a break.

Are you one of those women who can't go to bed at night without every dish washed and every load of laundry done? Give up perfectionism and give into more time for yourself. Does your house really need to be spotless? Your office need to be perfect? It's ok to leave some things undone while you take time to renew yourself. In fact, it's these kinds of short breaks that give you more energy to complete the tasks in front of you. There will always be more work to be finished, more cleaning to be done, more clothes to be washed. But if you continue to allow these things to take priority over time for yourself and your life, when will you ever have time to focus on you and your health and happiness? Remember, you only get one chance at life. You'd better enjoy it while you have it!

You have to be brave enough to challenge the voices in your head that tell you you're shirking your responsibilities or that you shouldn't be taking this time for yourself. I have learned real quickly that the dishes will still be there tomorrow, that I can find an alternate outfit to wear than the one sitting in the pile to be washed, and that the refrigerator will not go on strike if it's not cleaned today. Realize that things don't have to be perfect in order to give yourself a much-needed break. The world will not stop if you take 15 minutes for yourself. If you're still not sold, think of it this way—even God rested on the Seventh day (and you don't think He still had work to do?!)

Secondly, you need to start setting some new boundaries on your time. Many times we over-schedule our lives because we can't say 'no' or we don't want to miss out so we try to do everything. Taking on too many responsibilities is one way we begin to lose ourselves. Do you ever find yourself saying 'yes' to commitments you wish you'd said 'no' to and end up feeling resentful about it? That's a regular habit for many women.

Nothing drains your life of meaning more than saying 'yes' to doing something that your heart simply is not into.

Many women struggle with the need to please everyone. We can't do everything everyone would like us to do. Trying to be all things to all people puts us on the fast track to burnout. I used to have a hard time saying 'no' because I never wanted to disappoint people. But what I learned was that in doing that, the person I was continually disappointing was myself. My life changed when I understood that I don't have to keep everybody happy. If you live your life just trying to please people, you will eventually lose yourself in the process. You've got to learn that saying 'no' to some things allows you to say 'yes' to more time to take care of yourself. Your priorities should come first before saying 'yes' to other commitments because in your life you have seniority over other people's demands. When you learn to say 'no' to more things, it's actually a sign that you're growing in maturity. You are realizing that you can't do everything or you'll wear yourself out. Saying 'no' can be so refreshing. Learning to say 'no' will improve your ability to manage your time and care for yourself.

Thirdly, taking control of your schedule also means you need to learn to share the burden of your daily responsibilities with people around you. When we learn to delegate, we free up time to focus on our care. In fact, sometimes the best things we can do, for others and ourselves, is to step aside so someone else can step up. Perhaps it's a volunteer position that you can release to someone else or maybe it's some household chores that you can delegate to your children to help them grow in learning skills. Maybe there's a teenage neighbor that would love the opportunity to mow your lawn to get some work experience. Perhaps there's another woman who would enjoy cleaning your home to get a little extra cash so you can have more time for you. Look around your life and find areas that you can delegate so you can free up some time.

Yes, we have many responsibilities in life, but that includes a responsibility to ourselves and our own care. You may feel like you need to do everything, but the truth is—you don't! Sure, we may disappoint some people when we make choices to put ourselves first for once, but that is part of being fully present for your life. Remember, you must first be there for yourself before you can be there fully for other people.

I understand that the demands on your time are probably overflowing each day. So many of us look at downtime as a reward for getting everything else done on our to-do list. But time for yourself needs to be a priority, not a reward. In fact, the more pressures you face daily, the more you need to relax! You get to a point where you don't do anything effectively when you're so burned out. Would you drive your car nonstop without ever getting an oil change? Of course not! So stop driving yourself to the brink of exhaustion and start scheduling some time for you. I would guess you're about due for a break, aren't you?

Grounds for Thought: What hinders you from taking more time for yourself? Do you give yourself and your time away too easily? Do you find yourself saying 'yes' to many things you wish you would have said 'no' to? What things are you currently doing out of guilt or obligation? Are there responsibilities you can delegate to someone else that can free up more time for you?

Grounds for Action: Start making time for your life. Schedule at least 15-30 minutes each day for yourself. Start evaluating your daily routine and figure out the things you are doing out of guilt or obligation. Do you need to resign from a volunteer position, delegate household tasks better with your kids and/or spouse, or get rid of your perfectionist tendencies and allow yourself to leave something unfinished while you take a break? Or do you need to start saying 'no' to more things? Set some boundaries on your time.

JAVA JOLT #3:
Savor Some Solitude During Your Breaks

"Be still and life will bring you the answers." Neal Donald Walsch

When's the last time you gave yourself your own undivided attention? Let's face it, our jam-packed days are filled with constant noise from kids to co-workers to emails to phone calls to washing machines to the dog to TV—leaving very little time for quiet. Disconnecting from the noise of life is necessary for creating a healthy, happy life, but unfortunately, most women find this to be a difficult process. So many of us fear any kind of alone time. In fact, most of us fill every moment just so we don't have to be alone. But being apart from others, enjoying time in solitude, is what leads you to reconnect with the woman inside. Alone time allows you to distance yourself from the voices around you so you can start to hear your own. When your mind and body are exhausted and your life is filled with noise around you, you can't possibly hear the desires of your heart. If you want to refill your whole self—your mind, body, and *soul*, you need to give yourself times of solitude during your downtime.

Most of us have turned from human beings into human doings. We become so addicted to doing that we forget how to just be. Not many people know how to just 'set' anymore. But it's truly one of life's greatest arts. It's what creates space for new thoughts, ideas, and desires to surface. For most of you, the only time you ever give yourself silence is probably in the shower, and I'm guessing that most of your good ideas come in the shower, right? There's a reason for that! Research shows you get your best ideas at times when your mind is at rest. This is something others have known for years. I think you'll find this story interesting.

Second Cup Story:

Henry Ford (the founder of Ford Motor Company) once said he didn't want executives who had to work all the time. He insisted that those who were always in a flurry of activity at their desks were not being the most productive. He wanted people who would clear their desks, prop their feet up, and dream some fresh dreams. His philosophy was that only he who has the luxury of time and quiet can originate a creative thought.

So if you are feeling stuck and long to hear the desires of your heart, your solution is not in doing more, but in taking a break from the noise and busyness of life. When we give ourselves the gift of solitude during our downtime, fresh insights for our life begin to flow through us. It's where we can find the answer to questions like, *"What do I want?"* and *"How do I want to live?"* and *"What am I meant to do with my life?"*

I love sharing my story when people ask how I came up with the idea for The Inspirational Coffee Club. I was enjoying an Inspirational Coffee

Break one evening, alone, relaxing by my fireplace (coffee in hand) and a flood of ideas filled my head. One, after another, after another. I remember grabbing my notebook and just writing and writing and writing. And when I was done, I had scribbled out the entire *12 Ground Rules for Life* on a tablet of paper. I'll never forget the realization that hit me that night. A true epiphany and proof of what happens when we finally slow down long enough to give ourselves time to think. What would have happened if I'd just kept up the pace I had been going? That night I learned the importance of quiet, of stepping back from life in order to listen. I learned the value of solitude to hear what I needed to hear. Now I know better than ever that times of quiet and peacefulness are what allow us to access our inner wisdom and allow God's direction for our life to reveal itself.

Most of us have spent so many years asking other people's advice on our lives—on how we should live and what we should do. When we look to others for advice, we get drawn down *their* path. What's right for them is not best for us. That's why so many of us feel so empty: stressed, lost, confused, unsatisfied, and unhappy. To find our own way, we need to look inside ourselves. We need to find our own answers to make sense of our lives. When we shut out other voices, we gain clarity about who we really are and what we really want. You cannot have a complete sense of who you are until you can also savor some alone time to simply be with yourself. It's in solitude where you begin to hear the inner, deepest desires of *your* heart, not the desires of everyone else around you. Take time in your life to pause, find a quiet space to allow an opening for growth, and reconnection with your inner self.

So how can you create some peace and quiet in your life? There are numerous ways to find solitude during your busy days. Perhaps you can get up 15-30 minutes earlier than your family to enjoy your first cup of coffee in silence before others awake, or put the kids to bed 15 minutes early so you can enjoy a quiet cup of tea or a relaxing bubble bath before bedtime, or you could go for a 20-minute walk alone to watch the sun rise or set. Throughout the day, you could take your lunch to a park, sit in a corner of your favorite café, or sneak away to a favorite coffee shop down the street. Yes, there are other people around, but you can still be alone with your thoughts. Coffee shops can be wonderful places to sit and think. In fact, I've had many ideas spill out of me while having coffee at my favorite spots.

My all-time favorite strategy is creating your own Inspirational Coffee Break spot right in your home where you can go to relax and be alone—a place that no matter what's happening in your life you can find solitude whenever you need to. A place where you can withdraw from the demands of life to be alone even if only for a few minutes. It may be a corner of your bedroom, a room in the basement, a nook off the kitchen, or even a small spot in your walk-in closet. Even your bathtub or garden can be your sacred coffee break spot. Any spot that you can claim as 'yours.' If it's a place inside, decorate the spot with your favorite candles, pictures, quotes, flowers, lamp, and pillows. Or if it's the bathtub, buy your favorite scented bath salts or bubbles. Then, shut the door, turn off your phone, the TV, the Internet and e-mail, put a sign on the door that says, 'Do Not Disturb-Inspirational Coffee Break in Progress,' and do whatever it takes to keep your space sacred. Every woman should have her own Inspirational Coffee Break spot. You may even think of more creative ways to quietly step back from your frenzied world like this woman did.

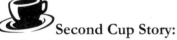**Second Cup Story:**

I read about a woman who was desperately craving some alone time; when her husband and young sons asked her what she wanted for her birthday, she jokingly said, *"My own deer stand."* The day of her birthday, her family led her blindfolded into the back yard and when they removed the blindfold, she looked up at the large tree in the yard and in sweet six-year old handwriting she saw a sign that said, 'Mom's Dear Stand' (note the spelling). There was a ladder to climb into the stand and a pail that allowed her to hoist up her favorite books, magazines, and coffee cup. It became her treasured spot to sneak away for regular times of solitude.

Use a mixture of any of the above strategies to create your own daily Inspirational Coffee Breaks. The main element is to take a little time everyday to get quiet and clear your head. Mark off 15-30 minutes each day—be it morning, afternoon, or evening—to just spend some quality time with you.

I recommend once you master the habit of daily breaks that you try an extended Inspirational Coffee Break sometime, too. It is important to find ways to get extended solitary stretches once or twice a year. Maybe a weekend in the mountains or at the lake or a few days at a Bed & Breakfast or at a retreat. One of my best friends recently filled me in on a weekend she spent at a silent retreat. She said the experience was life-changing and she came back more refreshed and filled than she could ever remember. My retreats involve booking a weekend at a quaint Bed & Breakfast and catching up on some much-needed rest and daydreaming. I enjoy getting away to a place outside of my home where I can hang out for the weekend and do absolutely nothing but relax, think, read, walk, and drink unlimited coffee, of course! I can sit for hours, listening deeply to the quietness and if I'm lucky, enjoy the beauty of nature and wind whistling through the trees. I have been to some of the most beautiful, inspiring places and have enjoyed peaceful sunsets, invigorating sunrises, cozy fireplaces, beautiful rooms, soft robes, soaking in a tub of bubbles, moonlight upon the water, and watching bright stars overhead. Without fail, I always come back feeling like a new woman. My zest for living deeply refreshed. So if you are one of those women who does not take time away from work or family, I encourage you to start making it a priority. Your happiness depends on it!

It is so important to learn how to stop and experience life without constant distractions. Learning to be comfortable with downtime can at first be difficult. I think many of us are afraid of what these quiet times might reveal to us. Once you get used to it though, you not only learn to relax, but you learn so much more about yourself. You learn to enjoy your own company. You learn to re-connect with yourself so you can make better decisions—for yourself, your family, your job, and everyone around you. You need silence. A time to relax, a time to dream, a time to reflect and space to listen to your heart's desires.

Most of the time, you're probably surrounded by other people. So during your downtime, delight in every moment you get to spend time with just you. Alone time is when you recharge, get back to your center, and distance yourself from all the distractions so you can hear your own inner voice with more clarity. Even Oprah understands the importance of solitude amidst a busy schedule. I recently read that she takes 10 minutes in the bathtub each day and then on Sundays spends the day completely alone, giving herself time to reconnect from her busy week. There isn't a single one of us who doesn't need that time of solitude. Savor some of your own!

Grounds for Thought: When's the last time you had some real peace and quiet? Are you comfortable with downtime or do you try to fill your time with other things to avoid it? Have you gotten so busy 'doing' that you've gotten uncomfortable with simply 'being?' Do you have a special soul-nurturing space you can set aside just for you?

Grounds for Action: Develop your own daily renewal practice. Every day, savor at least 15-30 minutes of quiet time. Consciously make space in your life to be alone—a hot bubble bath, a walk in nature, a good book, a cup of tea or coffee in the morning. I also encourage you to create your own Inspirational Coffee Break space just for you. Decorate that space with your favorite candles, pillows, quotes, lamp, pictures, etc. You may also want to make your own 'Do Not Disturb-Inspirational Coffee Break in Progress' sign (or you can purchase one at www.theinspirationalcoffeeclub.com) so that your family knows when you want to be alone.

At least once or twice a year, give yourself the gift of an extended break away from your daily grind. Take a day or two and go somewhere peaceful, quiet, and rejuvenating. Taking time to slow down, renew ourselves, and reconnect with our inner wisdom is a powerful strategy in living a more fulfilling life.

JAVA JOLT #4:
Add a Jolt of Inspiration to Your Restoration

"Motivation is like food for the brain. You cannot get enough in one sitting. It needs continual and regular top ups." Peter Davies

Not all breaks are created equally. Once you commit to taking 15-30 minutes of quiet time for yourself each day, it is essential to learn how to make the most of this 'me' time. Don't just use this time for a break; use it to give yourself a boost. If you use them well, these times of solitude that already have a place in your day can be enough to keep you inspired and full. A true Inspirational Coffee Break should not only recharge your body, but it should invigorate your *mind* and *soul* as well. A little downtime will help you feel good for awhile, but Inspirational Coffee Breaks will help you feel full for life. Here's the key: *When you use some of this time to consciously invest in your happiness and well-being, you transform ordinary coffee breaks into Inspirational Coffee Breaks.*

In this world where negativity, busyness, and stress are recurring themes, it can be tough to remain encouraged and inspired for life. We don't stay full automatically. If we want to live a more fulfilling life, it requires an investment on our part. We need regular sources of inspiration and instruction to keep us on the right track, to help us become a better woman, to improve ourselves, to provide hope for our future, and to get re-inspired for the rest of our lives. It is essential to be reminded and filled with messages that refill our soul and inspire us to live more fully. Learning how to add a jolt of inspiration to your restoration can truly change your life.

I heard a quote once that said, *"You become who you have coffee with."* There is so much truth to that. I think about all the wonderful people I've 'had coffee' with over the years—all the interviews I've listened to, the books I've read, the magazines I've learned from. Over time, the wisdom and inspiration a person gains from these resources cannot fail to rub off on her. Learning from others is what makes us better. We can restore our minds and souls by drinking in inspiration from others around us during our downtime. There are so many resources overflowing with great ideas and inspiration—books, magazines, speakers, retreats, conferences, DVD's. These are all sources that provide ideas, insights, motivation, and tactics that will help us become better women. The time you give yourself for Inspirational Coffee Breaks allows you to fill your mind with positivity, motivation, and hope by reading and listening to material that allows you to broaden your understanding of yourself. Get a fun journal to record your thoughts, revelations, and insights. You need to be constantly growing and learning positive strategies you can apply to your life to help you become the woman you want to be. A true Inspirational Coffee Break is a combination of self-renewal and self-improvement.

How can you add some inspiration to your restoration? Inspiration comes in so many forms. I have a friend who loves to soak in her bathtub at night and read her favorite running magazines because those inspire her to be a better athlete. Yours may be praying, reading your Bible, or studying scripture over a cup of tea. Or, perhaps going for a walk and bringing along your iPod with music or interviews you uploaded months ago that inspire you. When you sit in the tub, you could read one of those uplifting magazines that have been collecting dust on your coffee table. When you take your morning coffee break, you could reflect on your life and write in your journal. Or spend time reading your new self-improvement book at a coffee shop. Watch the sun set while you meditate or pray. Or sign up to attend an upcoming Women of Faith weekend event or a local women's conference at your church. When you do these things, you come back refreshed, physically and mentally. And I assure you—that refreshment brings with it creative ideas and a new perspective on life.

On any given morning, you will find me alone—taking 15-30 minutes of quiet time for myself in my Inspirational Coffee Break spot, enjoying my first cup of coffee, filling myself up with something inspirational and positive: my newest Guideposts, Success, or Oprah magazine, a new self-improvement book, passages from my Study Bible, an inspiring interview, and so forth. I sit quietly, giving myself plenty of time for self-reflection and loving every solitary moment as I relax my body and refill my soul. This is the time when I gain many new insights about my life. It's a definite daily ritual I try to never miss. It sets me in the right mindset for the day, eliminating so much of the tension of life. I wouldn't be the same person without it. I wouldn't have near as much energy and optimism to face the day. People often comment how peaceful and relaxed I am although my life is busy and filled with responsibility. I just practice what I preach—a daily Inspirational Coffee Break.

There's no wrong way to take an Inspirational Coffee Break as long as you carve out quiet time, pour out your guilt, and give yourself plenty of time to relax and fill your mind with positive, uplifting sources that replenish you. Do whatever it takes to get re-inspired every single day so you can go back out into the world, come up with new insights for your life, and be your best self. Read those inspiring magazines that you subscribe to but never seem to get around to reading, listen to stories and interviews of other people and learn from them, gather more books that help you work on your life, or get together with your own Inspirational Coffee Club to share conversations about what you are reading. I think as adults we forget that personal growth and enthusiasm for life don't happen automatically. It's up to you to keep giving yourself a fresh boost of encouragement and motivation in order to become the woman you really want to be. Use your Inspirational Coffee Break time to take yourself on a path of personal discovery.

A great quote comes from motivational speaker Zig Ziglar. Someone said to him, *"Zig, motivation doesn't last."* And he replied, *"Neither does bathing. That's why I recommend you do it daily."* Staying uplifted and filled doesn't naturally happen on its own. When we fill our souls at the same time we're resting our bodies, we literally give ourselves a double jolt of invigoration for life! Inspiration is like caffeine for your mind. It places in you new revelations and insights about your life that can excite and energize you. And the effects last far beyond your break. Making Inspirational Coffee Breaks a regular part of your life will fill you back up so you can be your best, most wonderful self and experience all the best life has in store for you. It's a process that I hope doesn't stop once you're done reading this book. Never stop learning, growing, and becoming all you are meant to be. And remember, life is much more enjoyable when you aren't running on empty!

Grounds for Thought: When's the last time you filled yourself up with something inspiring or encouraging? Do you feel you have stopped growing? How can you create your own Inspirational Coffee Breaks for yourself on a regular basis? What sources do you draw inspiration from (studying the Bible, reading good self-improvement books, listening to or reading other people's uplifting stories, articles from your favorite magazines, attending women's conferences, etc.)?

Grounds for Action: Start taking regular Inspirational Coffee Breaks and commit to refilling your mind, body, and soul on a regular basis. Every day, carve out 15-30 minutes, find a cozy, quiet spot, and fill yourself with a fresh dose of encouragement. Use the chapters in this book as a guide to get you started on your Inspirational Coffee Break journey. When you have finished this book, be sure to find other inspiring sources. Make Inspirational Coffee Breaks a life-long habit.

Extra Jolt Challenge: Organize your own Inspirational Coffee Club of women and start enjoying Inspirational Coffee Breaks together. Center your discussions on the chapters in this book, but also share with one another things that have restored, inspired, or uplifted you lately—other encouraging books or articles you've read, stories you've heard of people who exemplify these Ground Rules, workshops or retreats you've gone to, strategies you've learned to improve your life, etc. Share resources that can help uplift and renew others. If you feel like you don't have anything to share, then that means you haven't been taking enough Inspirational Coffee Breaks! Start refilling yourself regularly so you aren't one of those women who leaves herself empty. Visit www.theinspirationalcoffeeclub.com for information on how to organize your own club.

The Last Cup

The foundation to living more fully begins with learning to take better care of yourself. Therefore, building a better you should be the first step in building a better life. It's time to make your own mind, body, and soul a high priority. You can't become the woman you aspire to become when you are constantly on the go. Of course, we want to do all we can for those we love, but we can't leave ourselves empty. To be a great mom, wife, friend, employee, and leader, you must be a good 'you' first. A refreshed mind and body makes you far more productive and healthy than when you are exhausted. Inspirational Coffee Breaks are essential for life because they allow you to step back from your life, take time to pause, reflect, relax, and refill. This is how you begin to create a life of meaning and a future brimming with passion and joy.

I know the real world can make it difficult to care for yourself to the degree you deserve. Raising children, managing your work and your household, and being responsible for aging parents can cause your 'self' time to be very low as we get so busy caring for everyone and everything. In fact, it can plain exhaust you to the point that when you finally do get a break, you don't want to take care of anyone—including yourself. But taking care of yourself leads ultimately to taking better care of all those around you. This happens automatically because your mind, body, and soul are interconnected and when you do good for any part of yourself, all parts benefit.

No matter how busy you may be or what responsibilities you carry, this simple Inspirational Coffee Break practice will have a beneficial effect upon you. It is an easy way to a refilled body, mind, and soul. Our days bring a flurry of activity. For many, our lifestyles can be downright demanding, not to mention stress-inducing. It's time to relax, take a breath, and consider that creating and maintaining a healthy life isn't about getting all the details checked off your list. Instead, it's about committing to a regular self-renewal practice so you can feel inspired, happy and whole again.

A restored body and an invigorated spirit are the foundation for a joy-filled life. Start taking short time-outs from the demands and responsibilities of your daily grind so you can start re-connecting with yourself again. If you insist on always being on the go, and never allowing yourself time to refill, you will go through life empty. Perhaps you're there and don't know it. You might have years of self-neglect to repair, so don't think one or two short Inspirational Coffee Breaks is all you need. Make renewing your body and soul a daily ritual for yourself.

You need to keep yourself at the top of your to-do list without feeling guilty. Take care of yourself as well as you do everyone (and everything) else. Give yourself some time to think, dream, relax, and most importantly, get re-inspired for the rest of your life. Your happiness and health depend upon it. You deserve to take regular Inspirational Coffee Breaks, and I'm guessing your break is long overdue. Claim yours now!

"When we truly care for ourselves, it becomes possible to care more profoundly about other people. The more alert and sensitive we are to our own needs, the more loving and generous we can be towards others." Eda LeShan

GROUND RULE #2

Be the Leader of Your Own Coffee Club ~ Believe in Yourself

"Love yourself first and everything else falls into line. You really have to love yourself to get anything done in this world." Lucille Ball

Stop Waiting to Be Nominated—It's Time to Appoint Yourself the Leader of Your Life!

"Don't limit yourself. Many people limit themselves to what they think they can do. You can go as far as your mind lets you. What you believe, remember, you can achieve." Mary Kay Ash

As you get older, are you gaining or losing confidence in yourself? Believing in yourself is a key part of having a happy, fulfilling life yet a recent survey revealed that 88% of people let a lack of self-confidence hold them back from living the life they desire. Are you one of them? Your base level of happiness is determined by how you view yourself and your life. In order to create the kind of happiness you want, you need to become the leader of your coffee club again. Stop waiting for someone else to nominate you for the position and realize it's up to you to take charge of your own life. It's time you learn how to become your own biggest fan again so you can start living life to the fullest. But that's not always an easy task.

So many women live far below their potential. As they go through life, they let their defeats and disappointments from their past lower the expectation for their happiness. They hold dreams and desires for a better life, but they settle for a mediocre life instead of believing they can create or deserve a more fulfilling one. You may have had more than your fair share of discouraging things happen to you over the years, but that doesn't mean your future can't still be great. Believing in yourself means trusting that your future is still full of potential, even if your life hasn't turned out exactly as you'd hoped. It's believing that your best days are not <u>behind</u> you; they are in <u>front</u> of you! There is much more in store for you than you are experiencing right now, but most of us let whatever has happened in our past limit us from experiencing all we can during our remaining years.

Who decides what you can and cannot do in life? It's you. You set the boundaries for your life whether you realize it or not. Somewhere along the way, you made decisions in your life about what you are capable of and that becomes the ceiling that controls you. We go through life trained like this elephant at the circus.

 **Second Cup Story:**

In training an elephant for the circus, trainers take a skinny rope, tie it around the elephant's neck and attach it to a stake in the ground. Anyone can see that this giant elephant could easily rip off that rope and tear that tent down with barely any effort, but the elephant doesn't even try to get away. Why? Because the elephant has been conditioned. The trainers tied the same rope to him as a baby when he could struggle all he wanted but could not get loose. Then, as the elephant gets older, he finally decides he's not capable of pulling the stake out. And once that becomes the definition of his identity, he doesn't even try anymore. He believes that's just the way it is so he accepts this limitation.

So many of us are like that elephant, confined in our own comfortable environment. We don't dare to try to bust loose. Instead, we settle for less than we desire because we don't believe we're capable of accomplishing more. We believe we have no other options. Many people live their lives within boundaries that exist only in their minds.

Have you set limitations like this on your life? Perhaps you don't see it as a limitation, but anytime you catch yourself saying, *"Well, this is just how it's going to be,"* or *"I could never do that,"* or *"It's always been like this,"* or *"It's too late for me,"* you are putting limitations on your life and your happiness. It's really hard to live more fully when you've already defined yourself as *"This is just the way my life is."* The truth of the matter is that what you've been is not nearly as important as what you choose to become. You are more molded by the future than the past. Happiness comes when you set higher standards for what you want in your life and you believe in yourself enough to go for it. There is so much more in store for your life! Are you settling, or do you believe you can have a better future?

Let this be a wake-up call if you are one of those women who has stopped stretching and believing in herself. It's time you realize that you can still rise higher and go further. Sure, you may have been knocked down many times in your life, but what matters is that you get yourself back up and start believing in yourself again. Being the leader of your own coffee club means that you put your whole heart into what you want to accomplish. People are defeated in life not because of lack of ability; instead, they do not wholeheartedly believe they can succeed. A major key to success and happiness is to pour your heart into life, giving it all you've got, holding nothing back!

"Every achiever that I have ever met says, 'My life turned around when I began to believe in me.'" Dr. Robert Schuller

You're a great woman! You need to start believing that again and set new, higher standards for your life. You cannot accomplish anything worthwhile if you keep limiting yourself. If you knew all you were capable of doing, you'd astound yourself. Consider this inspiring true story.

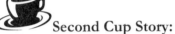 **Second Cup Story:**

Perhaps you've heard of famous comedian Phyllis Diller. There was a time in her life when she had very little confidence in herself. She was trying to raise seven young children on her own and at night worked as a custodian to make ends meet. One evening while she was emptying the garbage can of one of the big wigs, she saw a discarded handbook called, *'The Power of Belief.'* She took that home, read the whole book in one night, and realized she'd been thinking far too small for her life.

The book's advice was to find something you are good at, something you love to do, and do it with all your heart. She didn't really think she was good at anything, but as she thought about it more remembered that way back in high school people used to always tell her how funny she was. She had a gift for making people laugh. So one evening after her custodial shift was over, she went down to the local pub and signed up for a spot at open mike night. She was a hit. People loved her humor, and needless to say, the rest is history. Phyllis Diller has gone on to become one of the most famous female comedians of her day. She has said that her life changed the moment she started believing in herself.

Our beliefs about ourselves are the most telling factors in determining the level of success and happiness in life. How far you go in life will be directly related to how much you believe in yourself. When you believe in yourself, you stretch yourself. That's when you can begin to rise higher in all areas of your life. When you start to shift your confidence, you'll notice a significant shift in your life enjoyment. How you feel about yourself extends to every area of your life—your relationships, your work, and your personal happiness. You can go further than you ever thought possible, but it starts with boosting your confidence so you can bring out the best in the remaining years of your life. Inside of you flows greatness. Your best days aren't behind you—they are here and now and yours for the taking. They begin by appointing yourself the leader of your coffee club and believing you are worthy of a better future. Only then can you start to create the kind of life you deserve. Let me give you some strategies to give your confidence a boost.

Grounds for Thought: Are you gaining or losing confidence in yourself? Do you believe your best days are behind you or still in front of you? Are your expectations for your life and future too low? Do you need to set a higher vision for your life and your happiness? Do you believe you deserve to be happy or do you feel like you had your chance and blew it?

JAVA JOLT #1:
Refresh Your "Coffee Confidence"—It May Have Gotten Stale

"Nothing makes a woman more beautiful than the belief that she is beautiful."
Sophia Loren

How you feel about yourself is a determining factor in the enjoyment level of your life. Unfortunately, the world is filled with countless women who suffer from what I call low "Coffee Confidence." They are always finding fault with themselves: they rehash every mistake they've ever made, dwell on every regret they've ever had, and focus on everything they wish they'd done differently. In doing so, they tell themselves they are not deserving of more happiness or that they somehow are not good enough. Do not allow your faults and failures to trick you into believing you aren't worthy. No one has done everything right. We all have things we wish we could do over, but you can't allow past mistakes to keep you from being your best. No matter how many mistakes you've made, that doesn't change the fact that you are a wonderful woman who deserves to be happy. Start believing in your worth again!

The truth is, especially for women, that we constantly battle feelings of unworthiness—as moms, daughters, spouses, friends, and employees. No matter how hard we work at it, we never quite measure up to what we think we *should* be or do. Too often we judge ourselves unfairly and cut ourselves short. There's two main ways we do this. First, we're all too aware of our shortcomings, failures, unmet goals, and unmet expectations. Sure, you may have faults and you may have things you would like to change about yourself. Well, join the club. We all do! Quit being so hard on yourself. Here's the plain truth—you are entitled to make mistakes. No one is perfect. No matter how many mistakes you've made or what you've had to overcome, that does not change who you are. When you make mistakes, admit them and recognize them. Then forgive yourself, shake them off, and move on. Don't step into the trap of self-condemning.

Secondly, we damage our confidence even further by comparing ourselves to others and thinking that we'll never live up to their abilities or that we'll never be as good as they are. You should not be comparing yourself to others. You should be celebrating your qualities and your accomplishments. When we compare ourselves, it just drags down our self-esteem. If you're really going to be the leader of *your* coffee club, you need to quit comparing yourself to those around you. After all, they have their own club to head up. And believe it or not, they're most likely struggling with the same feelings you are.

Shake off guilt and inadequacies and start feeling good about who you are. Realize you are worthy just as you are. God created you—so essentially He was the founder of your club. Now it's up to you to be the leader and move forward with your life. Nothing you have done makes you any less loved in God's eyes. You will never be your most confident self when guilt and inadequacies still hold so much control over you.

"The greatest happiness of life is the conviction that we are loved -- loved for ourselves, or rather, loved in spite of ourselves." Victor Hugo

It makes very little difference for me to tell you how worthwhile and valuable you are unless you actually believe it for yourself. For most of us that means we need to start changing the way we see ourselves. Be honest—how often do you think about all the positive things you've done in your life? If I asked you to list 10 things you've done well over your lifetime, would you even be able to do it? If you're like most women, your mind probably gets stuck on all the things you didn't do right. We focus on our weaknesses and shortcomings instead of celebrating our accomplishments and strengths. You may do a hundred things right, but if you make one mistake that is what you remember. The negative experiences are what you remember the most clearly. As long as you stay focused on the negative, you will not feel good about yourself. Sure, you've made mistakes, but you've also done plenty of things right in your life. Don't get so stuck on all the things you didn't do right that you fail to see all the wonderful things you've accomplished.

It's time to start focusing on what you've done right so you can start feeling good about who you are. Research shows that the more you acknowledge your past successes, the more confident you'll become. Be proud of your past accomplishments. We all have them. Even the most minor achievements can be successes. Believe it or not, even your defeats in life can become positive if you choose to see them that way (i.e. bouncing back from a tough divorce, persevering through an unexpected job loss, getting adjusted to a new area after a job transfer, completing your first Bible study, losing five pounds, writing chapter one of your first book, etc). When you start to bring to light the successes you've had in your past, you gain a confidence boost for more possibilities for your future.

The only way you will create a life you love is with a committed, nurturing relationship with yourself. You have to appreciate and value yourself above anything else. Until you make peace with who you are, you'll never be content. Today can be a new beginning regardless of any past mistakes, regrets, or setbacks. You can make something great out of your life yet. The only way we can do this is if we have the right attitude about ourselves. We can't continue to wallow in our mistakes and expect to be a confident woman. You must rise up and start redeveloping your "Coffee Confidence." Learn to appreciate yourself and not compare yourself to anyone else. Decide to accept yourself unconditionally right now.

"Too many people overvalue what they are not and undervalue what they are."
Malcolm Forbes

Grounds for Thought: Can you say that you totally love and accept yourself as you are? In what ways do you most often feel unworthy? What mistakes, regrets, and decisions are you still beating yourself up over? Do you focus more on your shortcomings than your accomplishments? How often do you think about all the things you've done right in your life? Do you regularly compare yourself to other people and feel you don't measure up?

Grounds for Action: Give yourself a "Coffee Confidence" boost. In writing, make a list of at least five qualities you like or appreciate about yourself (kind, loving, thoughtful, hard-working, positive, persevering, nurturing, sense of humor, good listener, encourager, etc). Then make a list of five accomplishments you're proud of (friends you've made, relationships with your family, risks you've taken, contributions you've made to others, kids you've raised, challenges you've overcome, starting over after a divorce, bouncing back after a difficult loss, switching careers, surviving a layoff, paying off debt, achieving a goal). Make sure you keep this list and refer back to it often whenever you need to remind yourself of your greatness. In spite of what feels like is going wrong in your life right now, deep inside is a smart, wise, loving, and hard-working woman who is filled with greatness and has a history of past successes! Continue to add to this list as you move forward.

Now, it's time to celebrate yourself! Buy a fresh flower for yourself and attach a tag that reads, *'Thank you for being you!'*

Extra Jolt Challenge: Ask a few of your closest friends or family to tell you what qualities they most admire and appreciate about you. You can download Confidence Cups for free at www.theinspirationalcoffeeclub.com and email or hand them to friends to fill with qualities they most appreciate about you. Look at them every time you're feeling down about yourself.

JAVA JOLT #2:
Monitor Your Internal Coffee Talk

"If you think you can, or you think you can't, you are correct." Henry Ford

You have a constant companion around you 24/7 and rarely does she ever shush up. She is with you from the time you wake up until the time you fall asleep at night. She's the most relentless member of your coffee club, but sadly, she is often times the most unsupportive member as well. She often turns more into a critic than a loving companion, and unfortunately, she lives with you so there's very little chance of getting rid of her.

If you haven't guessed yet, I'm talking about the inner dialogue going on within ourselves throughout the day—something I call our internal Coffee Talk. Do you realize that we talk more to ourselves than we do anyone else? The question is: *How are you speaking to yourself?* Are you saying positive, affirming, empowering thoughts? Or are you saying negative, defeating thoughts? You have thousands of thoughts that go through your mind each day, and if you're like most women, the majority of those thoughts are negative. In fact, about 95% of what we stay to ourselves is negative. How can you possibly expect your confidence to increase when you speak to yourself this way?

If you listened to this internal dialogue going on inside of you, you'd find that you discount yourself the majority of your waking hours. Did you know that the average person disapproves of themselves over 50 times a day? We're continually putting ourselves down or comparing ourselves unfavorably to others by saying, *"What's wrong with me?" "I shouldn't have done that." "I'm such a klutz." "I'll never lose weight!" "I'm not that talented." "I should have done things differently." "I can't do anything right."* Over time, these thoughts start to accumulate. It's no wonder we don't have the confidence we should because we are constantly dwelling on negative thoughts about ourselves. I heard someone say that if we talked to our kids the same way we speak to ourselves, they'd call social services on us. What in the world are we doing to ourselves? Why do we constantly condemn ourselves when we're trying our very best?

I don't believe we're ever totally capable of silencing this negative Coffee Talk. After all, that inner companion is part of who we are. But the good news is that once you become aware of how you're speaking to yourself, you can gradually start to fix it. You can learn how to get better at monitoring your internal Coffee Talk and filtering out those negative, distasteful thoughts when they come to you. All day long, you need to be on the look-out for these self-defeating words and thoughts so that you can begin to filter those and replace them with words of self-approval. In essence, you have to teach yourself how to start talking more lovingly and compassionately to yourself.

Our internal Coffee Talk should always be positive and encouraging. We have to get out of the habit of thinking negative thoughts about ourselves. Stop saying, *"I'm so slow." "I'm unattractive." "I've failed so many times." "Who'd want me?"* SHUSH! Get those phrases out of your vocabulary. If you dwell on that talk, it will set limits on your life. After all, you believe what you say about yourself more than what you believe anyone else says. If you don't believe me, you can learn a good lesson from this story.

 **Second Cup Story:**

There's a story of a man and his young son who were hiking up a mountain. The little boy slipped, and slid quite a ways down the mountain side until he was finally caught by some brush. Unhurt, but frightened, he called out, *"Somebody help me!"* A voice called back, *"Somebody help me!"*

The boy looked surprised and confused. He said, *"Who are you?"* The voice shouted back, *"Who are you?"* The boy began to get aggravated. *"You're a coward!"* he yelled. The voice shouted back, *"You're a coward!"* The boy shot back, *"You're a fool!"* The voice repeated, *"You're a fool!"*

By then the boy's father had reached him and helped remove him from the brush. The boy looked up at his father and said, *"Dad, who is that?"* His father chuckled and replied, *"Son, that's called an echo but it's also called life."*

He continued, *"Son, let me show you something."* The dad shouted out, *"You're a winner!"* The voice shouted back, *"You're a winner!"* The dad's voice said, *"You've got what it takes!"* The voice boomed back, *"You've got what it takes!"* That dad shouted, *"You can make it!"* The voice shouted back, *"You can make it!"*

"Son, that's exactly how it is in life," the father explained. *"Whatever you send*

out always comes back to you."

Make sure you are speaking good messages about yourself. If you hear negative comments long enough they drop down into your spirit and they produce exactly what you are saying. That's why it's so important that we get into a habit of monitoring our internal Coffee Talk so we can teach ourselves to speak more lovingly to ourselves. Since you can't turn off this inner Coffee Talk, you have to learn how to re-direct it.

Start talking to yourself the way you'd talk to your best friend over coffee. Would you ever dream of telling her that *she's fat, she's unorganized, she's inadequate, she's unattractive, she's not a good mother, she's an idiot, she's not worth it, she shouldn't be happy, her dreams are silly,* or *she really screwed up this time?* Of course not! Yet, I'm guessing that you've spoken at least one, if not all, of these thoughts to yourself recently—most likely today. Extend the same kindness, gentleness, and understanding to yourself as you would a cherished friend. Cut yourself some slack and accept yourself just the way you are.

All through the day, teach yourself to dwell on positive thoughts about yourself. That's how your self-esteem is energized. When you get into the right habit of talking to yourself with positive, affirming thoughts, your confidence begins to rise. Instead of seeing yourself as a washed up woman, you will begin to see yourself as full of life and potential. As you consistently make positive declarations, this new attitude fills you and spills out into all other areas of your life.

Grounds for Thought: How do you talk to yourself when no one is looking? Do you speak more positive or negative thoughts to yourself? What feelings of self-doubt do you fight each day?

Grounds for Action: Start noticing how many times throughout the day you beat up on yourself or compare yourself unfavorably to others. Before you can change it, you need to become aware of it. Whenever a negative thought about yourself creeps into your mind (and they will), immediately cancel it out with something more positive. The more regularly you do this, the easier it becomes and the better you feel about yourself.

Train yourself to start talking to yourself more lovingly. Every time you look in the mirror throughout the day, say *"I am great!"* Keep saying it over and over, preferably out loud, even if you don't feel like you're great. You should say this to yourself at least 10 times a day. Soon you will notice that you are feeling better about yourself. Once you've mastered that one, start saying, *"Hello, good looking."* Not only will it make you smile, but in the long run, you will feel happier and more confident in yourself. The more you hold your head high and hold that positive image of yourself, the more your mind will actually begin to believe it. There's some truth to the saying, *"Fake it till you make it!"* If you're not feeling great right now, start telling yourself you are, and you'll soon notice a shift in your confidence and self-worth.

JAVA JOLT #3:
Choose the Members of Your Coffee Club Wisely

"A true friend knows your weaknesses but shows you your strengths; feels your fears but fortifies your faith; sees your anxieties but frees your spirit; recognizes your disabilities but emphasizes your possibilities." William Arthur Ward

As much as we hope to never get down and to never doubt ourselves, we are only human and self-doubt is going to rear its ugly mug. At times, we all need a little encouragement to keep us inspired throughout our journey. One of the most powerful strategies for keeping your confidence boosted is to have a great support system around you who encourages you and believes in you when you sometimes lose confidence in yourself. I call this support system your personal coffee club—a positive, uplifting community that challenges and inspires you to become the woman you want to be. It's critical you choose the members of your personal club wisely because who you associate with on a regular basis can make a huge difference on how fully you live. Let me explain with this example.

 **Second Cup Story:**

Did you know that certain species of fish grow according to the size of their environment? Put them into a small aquarium and they remain small. Release them into a natural body of water and they grow to their intended size.

People are similar. If you surround yourself with a limiting environment, you will stay small. But put yourself in an environment that encourages growth, and you will expand to reach your potential. Are you currently in the aquarium or the sea? Who do you want to have swimming with you? It doesn't matter how great your potential is if you aren't in an environment where you can grow beyond where you are right now.

There are people around us who encourage, support, nurture, and inspire us (caffeinated people) and there are those who discourage, shoot down our dreams, criticize, and leave us emptied (decaffeinated people). The most valuable members of your coffee club are those who raise you up, not bring you down. They are the ones who make you feel encouraged and inspired after spending time together (either in person or on the phone), not discouraged and defeated. They are the people who believe wholeheartedly in you and your potential and who truly want you to succeed and grow beyond your current limitations.

Take a close look at the people you currently have surrounding you. Do they help bring out the best in you? Do they increase your confidence or bring you down? If you're like most women, you do not come home to a cheerleading squad waiting in the driveway. In fact, it's often those closest to us that tend to discourage our dreams and give us regular 'reality checks.' So it's up to you to create your own personal cheer team for life.

Choose to associate with people who bring out the best in you and encourage you to strive higher. Those who help remind you of your greatness and see things in you that sometimes you don't see in yourself. Those who encourage you to move forward instead of trying to limit you. Those who help you focus on all your possibilities instead of continually reminding you of mistakes you've made in the past. Get around people who believe in you, accept you, encourage you, and give you the confidence boost you need to move forward.

"Call it a clan, call it a network, call it a tribe, call it a family. Whatever you call it, whoever you are, you need one." Jane Howard

It's amazing what we can accomplish when we have people who really believe in us. Most people will not reach their full potential without someone else believing in them and challenging them to reach for new heights. I wouldn't be where I am today without the wonderful support of my own personal coffee club. When I first began to consider starting a business, I had no idea where to start. I truthfully didn't know if I could do it. I wasn't a natural writer, speaking in front of big crowds made me nervous, and the idea of my own business seemed completely overwhelming. But I knew I had a big dream in my heart and a lot of life experiences to share. For awhile, I didn't tell anyone because I doubted myself and if I was really capable of pursuing such an endeavor. Over time, as I began to confide in those closest to me about my ideas and goals, I'd hear comments like, *"Julie, your ideas are awesome." "You have so much to offer." "You're going to be helping a lot of people." "If anyone can do it, you can."* Each one of these phrases still sticks with me and has helped lead me to where I am today. For that, I am so grateful.

Those closest to me saw things in me that I didn't see in myself. They kept offering seeds of encouragement which in turn gave me the confidence I needed to keep pushing forward. I learned something so valuable—*when people believe the best in you, they help to bring the best out of you*! When others believe in you so much, you begin to believe in yourself. Many of us simply need people who believe the best in us to help instill the confidence we need to do great things in life—no matter what our age!

In my life, I've been so blessed to have people who believed in me. But I've also had those who discouraged me and who were all too quick to give me a dose of reality. Those who told me this would be hard, that my dreams were too big, and that it's an awfully big undertaking for one person. Well, they weren't telling me anything I didn't already feel inside, but if I would have listened to those discouraging words, I'd never be where I am today. And you'd never be reading this book!

You never bring out the best in yourself around people who criticize you and try to discourage you. Unfortunately, our lives overflow with cynics, critics, and fault-finders. There are many people who quickly point out what we are doing wrong, but relatively few take the time to point out what we are doing right. Cherish those around you who build you up. Sometimes the best thing you can do is break away from negative people and surround yourself with more encouraging ones. Those who believe in you, encourage you, and inspire you to rise higher. Your life and your happiness depend on it.

I believe that every woman who is serious about living her best life should surround herself with her own Inspirational Coffee Club to help her realize her greatness. It's in there—you just need to get it out! Get around people who give you more confidence, help you grow, make you stronger, push you to be your best, and inspire you to become a better woman in all areas of your life. Inspirational Coffee Clubs come in all sizes and forms—whether it is an actual Inspirational Coffee Club of women that gathers regularly to study and apply these Ground Rules or just one close friend you can call to encourage one another over the phone.

Your environment can greatly affect your confidence and how far you'll rise in life. Get away from naysayers and surround yourself with yeasayers! Get around people who encourage you to grow, inspire you to improve, give you a gentle 'kick in the cup' to start living more fully, and cheer you on when you're doing well. Remember, you are the leader of your own coffee club. Therefore, you get to choose who you will surround yourself with throughout this journey of life. Choose the members of your coffee club wisely—your confidence, happiness, and success depend upon it!

"The size of the future you actually experience will largely be determined by one factor: people you choose to connect with. When you invite people who are truly committed to growth into every aspect of your life, your own potential for growth becomes truly unlimited." Dan Sullivan

Grounds for Thought: Are you surrounding yourself with loving, caring people who support, encourage, and inspire you to be your best? What kind of support do you get from your closest family and friends? Is there anyone in your life that discourages you or threatens to erode your confidence? Who around you inspires you to become a better woman? Who challenges you to think bigger for your life? Who do you have that's helping you grow, improve, and stretch to the next level? Who do you have to celebrate your accomplishments with?

Grounds for Action: Identify the people in your life who encourage and inspire you most. Who challenges you to want to be a better woman, to take more chances, and to pursue your dreams and desires? Who believes in you with their whole heart? Start spending more time with them, whether in person or by phone. Talk to those people regularly to gain encouragement. Then, identify who discourages you the most or is holding you back, and try to limit your time with them.

Extra Jolt Challenge: Organize your own Inspirational Coffee Club that meets regularly to inspire each other to live more fully by studying and applying these 12 Ground Rules together. Reach out to other women— amongst your friends, church, office, or family—and invite them to be a part of your Inspirational Coffee Club. We can learn so much from other women. When you get the support of other positive, nurturing, and uplifting women, you create a type of environment that will help you stretch in ways you never thought possible! Creating a network of support takes time, but it's time well spent.

There's an invigorating power in an Inspirational Coffee Club. It can truly transform your life. Imagine how it would feel if you had a permanent group of women who met frequently to energize your journey. It is amazingly empowering to have the support of a motivated and inspirational group of people where you can take turns sharing progress, encouraging each other with fresh, new ideas and offering some accountability and support. If you haven't organized your own Inspirational Coffee Club yet, get started! Remember, you don't have to go through life alone. We all need our own personal fan club to support our journey. And know this—I am one of yours!

The Last Cup

Although having others believe in you is very important, the single, most significant member of your coffee club is YOU! You must have a solid belief in yourself. A committed, nurturing relationship with yourself is essential if you are going to be successful in creating the life you most desire. Life will test you over and over until you feel confident about who you are. You need to believe in your worth more than anyone else does.

Stop waiting for approval from other people to start working on your life and happiness. Your confidence cannot come from anyone outside of you. It has to start from within. What you think of yourself has a much greater impact on your life than what anybody else thinks. Make the decision to become the leader of your club. Truly believe you are an excellent woman who deserves to live a life that overflows with fulfillment.

No one is born self-confident. It's something we need to continue developing every day. A prerequisite to living your best life is to love yourself first. Appreciate and respect the woman within. If you don't have a healthy respect for who you are—learning to accept yourself, faults and all—you will never be truly fulfilled. Your lack of self-confidence will begin to spill out into other areas.

Remember this—the best is in front of you! It's not too late for you and you most certainly are not inadequate. You are worthy of a great future. There's no limit to what you can still accomplish when you believe in yourself. See your potential, raise your expectations for your life, and most importantly, always have faith in yourself. You are extraordinary! Keep your confidence high, challenge yourself to rise higher, and you will discover that life keeps getting better and better. Your best days are not behind you; they are in front of you as long as you believe in yourself enough to reach for them!

"Nobody can make you feel inferior without your consent." Eleanor Roosevelt

GROUND RULE #3

Find Your Special Blend ~
Be True to Yourself

"Find your true path. It's so easy to become someone we don't want to be, without even realizing it's happening." Bernie Siegel, MD

Get Back to Your Whole Bean (not Ground Down) Self—It Makes Life So Much Richer!

"There is only one you. God wanted you to be you. Don't you dare change just because you are out-numbered." Charles Swindoll

One of the main statements I hear women say is, *"I don't even know who I am anymore."* We have so many roles (and not the ones around our side!). We play wife, daughter, sister, mom, friend, employee, and caregiver. That's in addition to chef, chauffer, and maid. It's so easy to lose ourselves in a world where we're getting pulled in so many directions. We spend so much time trying to manage work, social activities, and our households that it's common to find we have no idea who we are anymore other than what we are for others. If you're one of those who feels like you don't know who you are or what you want anymore, it's time to reconnect with your Special Blend. Finding your Special Blend means getting to know the real you again.

One of the reasons we begin to feel unfulfilled is when we're living a two-sided life. We're showing the world one part of us, but inside our heart we desire another. We push our priorities aside by doing what we 'think' we should do instead of what we really feel like doing. We are so trained to live in our heads, not our hearts. By doing this, we can be successful on the outside, but on the inside feel like a fraud. It's time you learned to reconnect with your heart and find that Special Blend inside yourself. One of the greatest responsibilities in living life to the fullest is to be true to yourself.

Second Cup Story:

I read an interesting story about Joy Behar, comedian and co-host of ABC's *The View.'* Did you know that Joy did not become a comedian until she was around 40-years old? Prior to that she had been an employment counselor, worked at a mental hospital, and taught English. She did everything she thought was expected of her. Despite all these wonderful roles she played, inside she still felt empty and incomplete. On the outside she looked successful, but on the inside she had this other little voice saying, *"You have to do what you want to do."* She always had in the back of her mind a desire she wanted to pursue since she was 10-years old—stand-up comedy. So that's exactly what she decided to do. She made some changes in her life to live more authentically and the rest is history; she's gone on to become a successful comedian and talk show host starting a new career mid-life.

How much more of your life will you allow to pass by without seizing control and making sure you are living true to yourself? You read so much about people who have a mid-life crisis or a medical scare, and afterward completely change their lives. It's usually because they finally realized they aren't living true to themselves. Don't wait for a mid-life crisis to start living life how you want to. (Or maybe you're having yours right now!) Stop trying to adapt yourself to be what everyone else wants you to be. Be an original. Be yourself. You *are* a Special Blend.

God freshly roasts each and every one of us. When we're born, we are born as our whole bean selves—the purest, richest form of ourselves. Our whole bean self contains our natural abilities, dreams, desires, values, and strengths. Sure, there are others who have the same talents as you, pursue the same dreams, feel the same desires in their heart, or hold the same values, but no one has exactly the same combination of those as you do. Just like a snowflake, there are no two Special Blends alike. That's what makes you your very own Special Blend. Your difference is what makes you priceless.

Over time, however, our whole bean selves become ground down by the expectations, demands, and intentions of others—the *'you ought to's,' 'you should's,' 'you need to's,' 'you'd better,' 'we think.'* Many of these requests come from well-intentioned loved ones, but before you know it, it's so easy to become a version of ourselves that we don't even recognize. Instead of being 100% authentically you, perhaps you're 30% what your spouse wants, 30% what your kids want, 20% what your parents want, and 20% what your friends want…so where does that leave you? How much of yourself is actually want YOU want? We often give up our sense of ourselves to other people because we are so quick to live up to someone else's expectations of us rather than our own.

It is so easy to become someone we don't want to be without even realizing it's happening. To start living life to the fullest, you need to get back to your whole bean self and start making decisions based on what you want instead of what others want. If you don't make time to get to know what you want, then others (family, work, community) will be happy to fill in the blanks. Then it gets to a point where it's not really your life you're living; it's theirs.

So who were you born to be? How do you know what you're meant to do with your life? What is your purpose? I get asked questions like these a lot. The answers are all inside of you. Unfortunately, we often look outside of ourselves for the answer to these most personal questions. We ask other people what they think we should do with our lives. No one can answer these questions but you. Just tune into your heart! If you start filtering out all the layers of your life, your Special Blend will be waiting. It's in you, just waiting to be rediscovered. Your Special Blend is what you bring to this world. When you reconnect with your Special Blend your life is infused with happiness and fulfillment. You begin to start living your life again in the way that brings you the most joy, and it makes your life come alive. Let me give you some suggestions for reconnecting with your Special Blend so that you can leave your mark on this world.

Grounds for Thought: Are you passionate about your life? Are you living life the way *you* want to be living? Who are you trying to please? What would you like to do if you stopped considering everyone else's expectations and opinions? Is the blend you're showing the world now really the one you want to be living for the next half of your life? If not, what changes do you need to start making?

JAVA JOLT #1:
Stop Comparing Yourself to Other Blends—It's Not Their Life You Want to Drink Anyway!

"You can't go around being what everyone else expects you to be, living your life through other people's rules, and also be happy and have inner peace." Dr. Wayne Dyer

We live in a world that loves to compare. We are all guilty of doing this. We have this mistaken notion that we should live how everyone else lives. However, if you are going to truly live your Special Blend, you cannot let others become the standard for your success and happiness. When you try to imitate others, your own life will soon feel empty. You can spend your life looking around seeing how others are living or you can find and live true to your own Special Blend. Your Special Blend comes from being the best 'you' possible. It doesn't come from trying to be someone else.

Being true to your Special Blend takes courage. Families, work, and society all have their own ideas of what we should do to be successful. So we need to make sure we're not living other people's dreams for our life. Yes, it can be challenging to be different, but true fulfillment comes when you are most true to yourself. Courage comes by believing you have the right to be who you are. You are not here for the approval of others.

Challenges to living our Special Blend are all around us. Perhaps all of your friends are having kids, and you don't have that same burning desire to be a parent, or maybe your neighbors have lavish gardens, and you can't even get the one potted plant in your home to grow, or your sister can whip up gourmet-tasting meals, and you can't even boil an egg, or you feel called to be a stay-at-home mom, but your boss has other plans for your future, or your parents want you to take over the family business or to go to law school, but you dream of something else. Do not feel guilty for not being more like others around you. You must stop worrying so much about pleasing others and start learning to please yourself.

We compare ourselves to others and think we should have the same desires and abilities as they do. Then when we don't, we allow ourselves to feel guilty about it or worse, we think there's something wrong with us and try to change. Don't try to be someone you are not. Remember this: you *are* a Special Blend—you aren't going to be exactly the same as your friends, neighbors, siblings, or co-workers. And you may not be exactly what your parents want you to be. But that's ok. Consider the story of Taryn Rose, a gutsy lady who made major changes to be true to herself.

 **Second Cup Story:**

Taryn Rose is a Vietnamese woman whose parents came to the United States in order to give their daughter more opportunity for her future. Growing up, Taryn always did what her parents wanted. And what they wanted most for their daughter was for her to be a doctor, and they told her this over and over while growing up. She obediently went to medical school and became an orthopedic surgeon—and a very good one! One of the best in her field, she was admired by other surgeons in fact. The only problem was that she felt dead inside. One day she envisioned her future and she saw herself doing the same 10 foot surgeries for the rest of her life and realized she didn't want to keep living like that. She took a good look at her life and asked the critical question: *"If I don't love what I'm doing now, when do I think I will?"* Taryn's head (and parents) were telling her one thing, but her heart and gut were telling her another. If she listened to her gut, she'd be going against what everyone else wanted. Yet she didn't want to be 60 and say, *"I wish I had done that."*

So she decided to make a change. But to what? Taryn wasn't passionate about being a surgeon, but she was passionate about helping women feel good about themselves. Taryn's patients had foot pain which meant they had to wear those special orthopedic shoes which were unattractive and unsexy. A lot of her patients said they'd rather suffer than have to wear ugly shoes. It bothered her that there wasn't a hot luxury shoe that was both comfortable and sexy. So she invented one and quit her job as a surgeon. Going from orthopedic surgeon to shoe designer was a big leap of faith and definitely not a good girl move. But that's what her heart was telling her to do. Her parents didn't speak to her for a year. They thought she was insane. Today Taryn Rose shoes are sold in over 500 specialty and high-end department stores internationally. And she loves her life (and her parents are talking to her again).

So many people feel like they have to live up to their family's expectations and those around them. Don't let anyone else shape you into who they think you ought to be. Make a commitment to yourself to not live your life around the approval of other people. The ultimate first step toward living your Special Blend is simply to make your decisions and live your life as you want to live it. Have the confidence to do what's best for you. Not what is best for your friends or relatives. It's a hard thing to do. But you can choose to live your Special Blend and be proud of it. Learn to leave behind the expectations of how others think you should be and what they think you should do. Inside of you is a Special Blend, waiting to be discovered and enjoyed. Your differences are a source of delight.

You need to find and live your Special Blend, but in doing so, be sure to not judge or criticize others for living theirs as well. Respect those around you even when they desire to live differently than how you do. You may want to be a career woman but all your friends want to be stay-at-home moms. Respect their decision as much as you do your own. You want to retire early to spend more time with your family while others want to work until they are older. Don't judge them for not making the same decision you do. You may want grandchildren but your kids prefer a child-free lifestyle. Support their decision even though it might not be the decision you'd desire. Remember, each one of us has our own desires inside our heart. It's unfair to try to pour our Special Blend onto someone else's life.

As we journey through life, we can either brew someone else's blend or we can embark on finding our own Special Blend and focus 100% on being our best selves. Focus on becoming the best *you* that you can be! Don't compare yourself to anyone else. Don't measure your success by anyone else's standards. Measure your success by the enjoyment you taste in your own life. Stop wasting your time trying to be someone else. Take the time to discover who you really are. Learn to love your authentic self. You are a Special Blend. Cherish that!

"Success is not the key to happiness. Happiness is the key to success. If you love what you are doing, you will be successful." Albert Schweitzer

Grounds for Thought: Are you pursuing the desires in your heart or are you drinking someone else's blend? Are you constantly comparing your life to someone else's? In what areas of your life do you compare most? Are you spending your life on things that please you? Or is most of what you are doing simply to please other people?

Grounds for Action: Start becoming more aware of the habit you have to compare yourself to others. When you catch yourself looking at someone else's life, STOP! Sit back, and ask yourself, what are the desires in your heart? Is this what *you* want? After all, you are the one who has to live with yourself.

JAVA JOLT #2:
Reconnect with Your Natural Ingredients: It Gives Your Life Its Fullest Flavor

"As you become clearer about who you really are, you'll be better able to decide what is best for you—the first time around." Oprah Winfrey

Each of us is born with a mixture of God-given qualities: dreams for our life, desires in our heart, talents unique to us, and abilities we excel at. Essentially, these are the core ingredients that make up our Special Blend. These are the elements of our life we should be using and pursuing everyday to create our richest, most enjoyable brew. Unfortunately, many of these qualities and traits get buried throughout our lives, and we end up using a blend that leaves a bitter, unfulfilling taste in our lives and hearts. We start to use whatever ingredients are easiest to find or ones that other people tell us to, hoping they provide the richness we're looking for. But until you start using the ingredients in sync with your Special Blend, your life will continue to lack the flavor you so deeply desire.

I already know what some of you are thinking, *"I don't even know what I'm good at!" "I don't know what I'm passionate about anymore."* The answers are all inside of you! Stop looking outside yourself to answer these questions. We become so used to tuning out the desires of our hearts that we don't even recognize them. It's time to do your part in digging them out and begin using them again. Let me use the following story to make my point.

 **Second Cup Story:** Acres of Diamonds

Years ago, when the first diamonds were being discovered in Africa, diamond fever spread across the continent like wildfire. Many people were striking it rich and becoming millionaires overnight. At this time, a young African farmer was scratching out a modest living on the land he owned. However, the promise of great diamond wealth excited the farmer so much that one day, when he could no longer restrain his desire and lust to become a wealthy man, he sold his farm, packed a few essentials, and left his family in search of the gleaming gems.

His search was long and painful. He searched day after day, week after week, but found no diamonds. He became sick, penniless, and utterly discouraged. Finally, worn out and feeling there was nothing more to live for, he threw himself into a raging river and drowned.

Meanwhile, the man who had bought his farm was working the soil one day and found a strange-looking stone in the small creek that ran across the property. He bent down and picked up the stone, admired it, and brought it home and placed it on the fireplace mantel.

Several weeks later, a visitor came to the farmer's home and noticed the unusual stone. He grasped the stone quickly and shouted excitedly at the farmer, *"Do you know this is a diamond? In fact, it's one of the largest diamonds I've ever seen!"* Further investigation revealed that the entire farm was covered with magnificent diamonds.

The farm the previous farmer had sold turned out to be one of the most productive diamond mines on the entire African continent. The first farmer had owned free and clear … acres of diamonds. But he had sold them for practically nothing in order to look for them elsewhere. How sad that he had not taken the time to investigate what he had right at his own fingertips.

Each of us, at this very moment, is standing in the middle of our own acres of diamonds. If we had only had the wisdom and patience to explore ourselves, we would most likely find the riches we seek. Our seeds of opportunity are usually in what we already know and what we are already doing. You can only find your ingredients by looking inward. Don't try to find fulfillment outside yourself. The ingredients of your

Special Blend are right under your nose. Don't be like that farmer and fail to see your acres of diamonds.

Our acres of diamonds are all the talents, abilities, dreams, and desires we were born with. We almost miss our God-given ingredients because we are so close to them. So much potential has been poured into you! You have great gifts inside of you that you might not even realize are there. Those gifts will be with you until the day you leave this earth. It's up to you whether you tap into them and use them or not.

When you find one of your talents or interests, use it and develop it as best as you can. Your natural interests may be music, inspiration, motherhood, counseling, sales, shopping, fitness, teaching, communications, athletics, crafts, quilting, finances, cleaning, coffee, children, elderly, speaking, sympathizing, cooking, healing, or assisting. Your natural talents might be working with animals, cooking, crunching numbers, singing, sewing, making people feel beautiful, making people laugh, making people feel inspired, your outlook on life, your sense of humor, your ability to make people feel special, organizing, or educating.

Learn to use and appreciate the skills, abilities, and gifts in which you are naturally talented. Recognize your strengths and choose to fill your life with activities that most suit you. When you are using your natural strengths you'll be happier because you are doing what you are naturally good at. I have to admit that writing this book, although a great sense of accomplishment, has included much anxiety and even some tears of frustration because writing is simply not one of my God-given strengths. Speaking—yes. Inspiring—yes. Writing—no. So I haven't had near as much fun writing as I do when I'm in my more natural environment of speaking, coaching, and inspiring.

"As simple as it sounds, we all must try to be the best person we can; by making the best choices; by making the most of the talents we've been given." Mary Lou Retton

Uncovering your natural strengths and abilities is indeed, one of the most important insights into your Special Blend. Yet, the world is filled with people who excel at what they are doing, but still feel so empty and unfilled. How can this be if they are doing things they are naturally good at? Well, you need to remember that your strengths and abilities are only one part of your natural ingredients. The other is your natural born dreams, desires, and passions. If you aren't combining both, your brew will leave a bitter aftertaste. We can be naturally good at something and still not enjoy it. Consider the story of this famous woman.

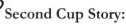 **Second Cup Story:**

Today, Aretha Franklin is hailed as the Queen of Soul. She has natural-born singing talent. But when she signed her first deal with Columbia Records, they tried to turn her into a pop jazz singer. Aretha was less than enthusiastic—her natural desire was to sing soul, not jazz. In 1966, she changed record companies, telling Atlantic Records that she wanted to focus on singing soul. They agreed, and after that, her career began to soar. She was one of the first women to actively steer her own recording career. Her mantra with producers was, "If you're here to record me, then let's record *me*, not you." As a result, she earned RESPECT.

Aretha is a talented singer. But her natural abilities and talents are only one piece of her inner ingredients. As you see from her story, a person can be naturally talented at something and not be passionate about it. The most common mistake people make is doing something just because they are good at it, but you also need to have a genuine excitement towards what you are doing or you will eventually lose your enthusiasm. Make sure that whatever you are doing, you are not only good at, but that you are also passionate about. When you can combine the two, life becomes so much more enjoyable. Talents come from your head, but passions come from your heart. You need to combine both your head and your heart to be fully happy. If your life is not a joy, maybe it's time to look at some new options that combine both your strengths *and* your passions.

So how do you know what you're passionate about? It's not as difficult as you think. It has to do with what excites you. What do you love doing? What desires fill your heart? What can you spend hours doing and lose track of time? Discover your passions by looking back over your life for those moments that make you come alive. Most of us can't see what's right in front of us.

From the time I've been three-years old, I've loved coffee breaks. It started when my Grandma taught me how to dunk sugar cookies into my coffee as a youngster and the addiction just stuck! As a teenager, I got my first job at a local coffee shop and loved every minute of it. My favorite hobby to this day is enjoying coffee with my family and friends. During college, I become interested in personal development books and inspirational speakers. In fact, I'd take my books and a journal and sneak away to my favorite coffee shops and spend hours immersed in reading inspiring stories, personal growth books, and uplifting magazines. To me, reading these kinds of materials seems almost like a hobby. I am passionate about it and the time just flies by. Looking back, I see now that this love of coffee and my personal growth is part of my destiny. Those desires were special roasted in me as part of my Special Blend.

If you are not fulfilled, you probably are not tapping into your natural passions. Make sure you are fulfilling the desires in your heart, tapping into the potential inside you, discovering what you do best, and what you do naturally. Explore your own interests. Whether it's a biking excursion or a pottery class or cooking class, every new pursuit has the potential to bring out your Special Blend so that you feel a greater sense of yourself. This may seem like a no-brainer, but it's sad how few people actually pursue any of their own desires. They work all day, they come home, make supper, take care of their families, do a load of laundry, they watch a little TV or talk on the phone, and then it's time to go to bed. Then they wake up the next morning and do it all over again. Where in that day did they take any time to pursue the things they enjoy? And we wonder why we feel so unfulfilled? Are you one of those women?

You need to have a sense of self outside of your marriage, your kids, and your job. Go out and explore some of your natural strengths and desires. In doing so, you become happier and more fulfilled and your family will notice a change in you. Reconnect with what really makes you happy. What things do you absolutely love to do? What things make time fly for you? Incorporate at least one of these things into your life each week—whether that be dancing, running, mentoring, enjoying coffee at a coffee shop, baking, sewing, horseback riding, painting, or cooking. Can't even remember what you enjoy anymore? Try this…what things did you love doing as a kid? Reading, riding bike, playing with pets, baking? Our childhood was our purest form and often gives great insight into what we love to do.

"People rarely succeed unless they have fun in what they are doing." Dale Carnegie

If you haven't yet stepped into your Special Blend—if you're doing many things for which you have little passion and enthusiasm—it is time to start being a better you. Examine your life. Be more aware of how you are spending your time. Are you doing what you are good at naturally? And more importantly, are you doing things that make you feel alive? If not, make some changes. Life is too short. Start making better use of the natural ingredients God has given you.

Don't live with your Special Blend undiscovered and don't die with all your ingredients still inside you. A lot of people die full. Full of their dreams, full of talents, full of ideas and interests, full of skills, and full of abilities that they never reached for. They never used them or pursued them. Do you know that most people only use 10% of the abilities they were born with? That's 90% untapped! Don't let this happen to you. Drink in life so fully that when you get to heaven you'll be able to say you've brewed everything you've been given!

"Most people go to their graves with their music still inside them." Oliver Wendell Holmes

It is our responsibility to continue to find fresh ways to use the gifts, talents, and strengths God has given us. You have many ingredients inside your head and your heart that work together to bring out the perfect roast. Your natural ingredients are the key to finding your purpose in life. Once you are clear on what brings you the greatest enjoyment, you will have major insight into your life purpose. When you are truly enjoying and pursuing the desires of your heart, you are on the right path to being true to yourself. Let me share with you one more great story to demonstrate.

 **Second Cup Story:**

A man and his wife were soon expecting their second baby. During one of the clinic visits, the man started talking to the doctor about what he did for a living. The doctor confided in the man saying, *"I wish I had been a musician because I love to play the piano."*

Soon after the visit, the man's wife had to have an emergency cesarean operation. After the delivery, the doctor came out with the good news that the man had a baby girl and his wife was going to be just fine. Another doctor who had assisted in the surgery walked up to the physician and said, *"Excuse me, doctor; I just wanted to tell you that you performed brilliantly in there, and it was an honor to assist you."*

When his colleague left, the man turned to the doctor and said, *"Now tell the truth. You have just brought a new life into this world, saved another life, and you've had one of your colleagues tell you it's an honor to work with you—for heaven's sake, can you honestly say you wish you had been a musician?"*

The doctor grinned and said, *"I was pretty good in there, and I know exactly why; this morning, I got up early, and, for one hour, I played Chopin on the piano."*

When you nurture and use your natural ingredients, it causes a fulfillment to overflow into the rest of your life and it affects everything else you do. One of the quickest ways you can pour your heart more fully into life is to make time for the things you love because when you are doing what you love, you are serving the world in the way you were designed to—with your own Special Blend. So go on, brew up the blend God has placed in your heart.

Grounds for Thought: Can you honestly say that you are regularly pursuing things that excite you? What unique gifts, talents, and skills do you bring to the world? Are there ways you can make better use of these resources? How can you incorporate more of your natural ingredients—your talents and your passions—into your current lifestyle? Are there desires that God has placed in your heart that you haven't pursued? Are there talents you have been given that you aren't using?

Grounds for Action: Sample some of your passions and interests. Make a list of your strengths, talents, desires, and interests. What are some things you love so much that you'd do for free? Think back over all the things you've done in your life and what makes you most happy? What can you spend hours doing that time just flies? Find one thing you are passionate about and start pursuing it. Find a way to infuse your passions into your daily life.

JAVA JOLT #3:
Decide How Your Coffee Can Will Read When You're Gone

"What we are is God's gift to us. What we become is our gift to God." Eleanor Powell

Our life and abilities are a gift from God but how we use them is our gift to God. Once you have recognized the unique gifts you've been given, it's time to figure out how you will use them to leave your mark on this world. What do you want your life to accomplish? What will be your greatest contribution to others? Taking time to figure out who you are, what you stand for and what you want to be remembered for is one of the most important things you can do to live your Special Blend. Building a legacy worth leaving behind begins today.

As you've learned, you have a Special Blend unique to you. But the interesting thing about this is that it's not designed only for *you*. It's designed so that you can share it with others and make a positive impact on the world. It's up to you to take what you have to offer and make the most of it. How will you use your natural ingredients—your gifts, talents, and desires—to leave the world a better place? The great thing about this life is that we each get to decide how our Special Blend will be used and remembered.

Before it's too late, it's crucial to be clear on what impact you want to leave on the world. What characteristics and attributes do you hope friends, family, and co-workers will say about you when you're gone? What do you want to be 'known for?' These essentially are the core values with which you should live your life *now* in order to be remembered for when you're gone. They should become the foundation of your Special Blend. It's important to decide the impact you want to have and the way you want to be remembered *before* you get to the end of your life and it's too late. The end is not the time to figure out how you want to be remembered. Today is when you need to start acting like that blend you want others to remember.

"The way to gain a good reputation is to endeavor to be what you desire to appear." Socrates

If you really want to know how to live your life, think about what you want people to say about you when you're gone and live backwards. Begin with the end in mind. Picture yourself walking down the coffee aisle in the grocery store. You get to the canister of coffees and you find the one that says 'Your Blend.' Inside that canister contains all the elements of your life—your qualities, your values, the dreams you pursued, the impact you made, and the way you lived life. The outer label defines what your life is all about. So what do you want yours to say?

Instead of a Flavor Scale, your canister has a Life Scale registering how fully you lived life. Where would yours register—Weak, Mild, Bold? And above that is the inscription of your life (your reputation) summed up in a few words. What would yours read—*wonderful wife, loving mom, great friend and good listener, inspiration to many, lived each day to the fullest, fun-loving and kind, devoted Christian, always made a person feel special, strong and persevering, got everything done but died anyway, crabby and negative, worked all the time, always exhausted, too busy for friends, always cranky, award-winning executive, a real pain in the butt, never took a vacation?*

Decide what kind of person you want to be. Then remember, to build the kind of reputation you wish to have, you must start acting that way. Actions speak louder than words. Is the way in which you've been living your life, the way you want to be remembered? Perhaps you need to start shutting down your computer and spending more time developing your relationship with Christ. Or maybe you should put down the dust rag or iron and pick up the phone to call a friend. Or turn off the TV and use it as a prop to make a fort in the living room in order to spend time with the kids instead. Look at the big picture of your life. If someone looked at your life from the outside, what would they see? You don't want to completely miss what you'd like others to see.

The day will come when our obituaries will be written. Others will review our lives and summarize what they saw in a few short words. We will have left our mark, and it will be too late to change it. The challenge now is to live as you'd like to be remembered should you not see tomorrow. In later days, when people reminisce about your life, what will they remember? As long as you are still living, your mark on this world is still being made. There is still time to change the way your coffee can will read when you're gone.

No matter what your situation in life, no matter what your gifts or talents, you can leave a beautiful legacy to impact those around you. We only need to willingly put to good use those gifts that God has entrusted to us to impact others. At the end of your life, don't question, *"Did I matter?"* Instead, decide how you want to be remembered, and then use what you've been given to leave a positive impact on someone else. Then, you'll *know* you mattered.

Grounds for Thought: What kind of legacy are you leaving for those around you? What three words do you think others would use to describe you? Is the reputation you have now the one you want to be remembered for? What do you want others to say about you when you're gone? Do you feel that you matter?

Grounds for Action: Create your own label for your legacy. How do you want your coffee canister to read when you're gone? If your life had to be summed up on the front of a coffee can, what would it say? Don't leave it to chance. Design your blend now. What kind of legacy do you want to leave?

My Coffee Canister:

At the end of your life, if you had to sum up how you lived life on the Flavor Scale, what do you want it to say? *Weak   Mild   Bold*

At the end of your life, if you had to sum up the three most important qualities you want others to remember about you (a description of your blend), what would they be?

Are you behaving as you want other people to remember you? What changes do you need to make in order to leave the kind of legacy you desire?

The Last Cup

Wake up and discover who you really are! The world is waiting for your Special Blend. Just as coffee comes in so many forms, so do our lives. None is the same. Be proud of your uniqueness. Find out who you are and embrace it! You were made to be you and not someone else. We've all been given a Special Blend and it is up to each of us to brew up our best life. Most people go through life and never fulfill their true potential. Avoid being one of them. Spend time uncovering your Special Blend. The real source of fulfillment is discovering who *you* are. It is what provides personal meaning and a deeper satisfaction for your life and gives you a greater overall sense of your own worth. It defines who you are and what you want to become, what you do, and how you do it.

Take a stand for who you are. Stop being what you think everyone else wants you to be. When you get to heaven, God isn't going to be asking why you weren't more like your neighbor or Mother Teresa. He's going to ask why you weren't more like you. Are you living your best life or are you living someone else's expectations for your life? Brew up your gifts, talents, dreams, and desires within you. These qualities and traits might be buried deep within you, but your Special Blend is still there. You need to do your part to start digging it out. When we're living true to ourselves, enthusiasm flows from us.

If we are not moving toward our Special Blend, dissatisfaction will remain in our heart. So many people are feeling unfulfilled because they are not fulfilling their destiny. It is so tragic to come to the end of your life on earth and realize you have not really lived—that you haven't become what you were intended to be. You simply endured an average, mediocre life, living without passion and enthusiasm. You allowed your Special Blend to lay dormant and un-brewed.

Without living true to yourself, it's easy to go through life distracted, journeying through life but feeling like you're accomplishing so little and wondering if your live even matters. But when you find your Special Blend your life wakes up and has far more meaning! Living your Special Blend means you're doing what you love to do, doing what you're good at, and accomplishing those things that are most important to you. Live your life so fully that when your time on earth is up, you can say you lived, 'good to the last drop!'

"Everyone is born an original, but most of us die copies." Unknown

GROUND RULE #4

Take Control of Your Brew ~
Create Your Future

"The difference between great people and everyone else is that great people create their lives actively, while everyone else is created by their lives, passively waiting to see where life takes them next. The difference between the two is the difference between living fully and just existing." Michael E. Gerber

Life is Like a Pot of Coffee—It Really Is How *You* Brew It!

"Life is what we make it, always has been, always will be." Grandma Moses

I challenge you to see your life as a pot of coffee you are in control of brewing. That's right-YOU are the Lead Brewer. The pot is your life and it's in your hands, just waiting for you to create your ideal brew. God created you with your own Special Blend when He gave you life. Now it's up to you to take control of your brew and make the most of the life you've been blessed with. You get to choose if your life is brimming with a rich, hot, enjoyable brew or if you let it be filled with a cooler, less satisfying one.

We were given an amazing gift that I think most of us forget as we get older. It's the ability to design our lives the way we want them. You have everything you need to create the life you desire. Yet, a lot of people leave their future up to chance. They simply let things happen to them rather than being intentional about creating what they want. In fact, most people spend more time planning their vacations than they do planning their lives. Are you one of them? Have you really taken control of your life or have you been letting life get away from you? Going through life without a plan for your future is like trying to go on vacation without a map. How will you know when you get there if you don't even know where you're going? It scares me how many people aren't concerned about where their life is going. It's time to take back control of your brew. Maybe other women will leave their future in someone else's hands, but not you! Put your future into good hands—that being yours!

So what does it really mean to take control of your brew? It's about creating the richest, most satisfying life for *you*! It's living on purpose instead of simply going wherever life takes you. The most fulfilled, happiest women do things differently than the rest. They create the life that they want—they don't just fall into it. They are very decisive about what they want and they make it happen.

"The best way you can predict your future is to create it." Stephen Covey

If you haven't realized it yet, your life simply will not stay hot on its own. To have the kind of life that brings fulfillment, you have to make the investment and take the initiative in creating the future you want. We need to work at it if we want life to stay fresh and exciting. Our life will grow cold and stale if we don't purposely take control of our happiness. I don't want this to happen to you. You can brew up a better life for yourself. Most importantly, you can brew up the life you want to live.

The wonderful thing about your pot of life is that you can choose to brew up a fresh pot anytime! It's never too late to change. The brew you've had in the past does not need to be the same one you have in the future. You may not be able to do anything about your past pot, but you can do something about your future one. You still have possibilities to become the woman you really want to be. In fact, where you are going is much more important that where you've been. So don't let your life get cold and stale. You will feel so much more enjoyment when you take back control of your life. Quit looking back. It's time for a new brew!

"We are still masters of our fate. We are still captains of our souls." Winston Churchill

It may be easier to just go wherever life takes us, but it's not nearly as enjoyable as when we go where we take ourselves. Don't let others determine your quality of life—take charge of your pot yourself. Make a decision that you are not going to live an average, mediocre life. That's like drinking cold-lukewarm coffee. Instead, put yourself back in control of your future. Don't leave it to chance; create it. Live it like you want it. It's time to make a shift from 'letting your life happen' to 'creating your life the way you want it.'

Remember this: though you can't go backwards and make a brand new start, you can start right now and make a new ending for yourself. I challenge you to finish your life strong! From this moment on, take control of your brew. If you do, your life can become an extraordinary masterpiece. The following are important steps in learning how to take control and make it just that.

Grounds for Thought: Are you in the place you hoped or expected to be at this point in your life? Can you honestly say you know what you want and where you are going? Have you been taking an active or passive approach to your life? Last year, did you spend more time planning your life or planning your vacation?

JAVA JOLT #1:
Take Full Responsibility for Your Brew

"You must take personal responsibility. You cannot change the circumstances, the seasons, or the wind, but you can change yourself." Jim Rohn

There is only one person responsible for the quality of life you live and that person is you. If you want to feel more happiness, have a more exciting career, enjoy deeper relationships, have better health or more money in your pockets, *you* need to take personal responsibility in making that happen. You are not entitled to a great life simply because you are here. Happiness and fulfillment rarely, if ever, happen on their own. You have to create them for yourself.

But this is not an easy concept for most of us. It's usually so much easier to make excuses for our unhappiness or blame other people rather than make changes. Many of us are like this moaning dog.

**Second Cup Story:**
One day a man heard his neighbor's dog moaning on the front porch. So he approached the neighbor who was sitting next to the dog. He asked him why his dog was whimpering. The owner said, *"Because he's lying on a nail."* Then the man asked, *"Well, why doesn't he just move?"* To which the owner replied, *"I guess it doesn't hurt quite that much yet."*

So many of us are like that dog on the porch, moaning and groaning about our situations, but not doing anything about them. Think about it—what are some of the things in your life you've recently complained about? Your extra pounds, an unorganized home, an unfulfilling job, too little time for yourself, your checking account balance, not enough contact with your friends and family? Most of the circumstances we complain about are actually situations we can do something about but have chosen not to. So why don't we do something?

Most of us avoid change. It's uncomfortable to have to make changes. But the pain of change is much less than the pain of staying in mediocrity. If all you do is continue to complain about what you are dissatisfied with, your life is not going to get any better. If you want something different for yourself, you're going to have to take responsibility for making some changes. Are you in a job you don't like, a relationship that's unfulfilling, an unhealthy addiction, a weight that's holding you back, or a financial situation that is keeping you awake at night? How bad does the pain have to get before you do something about it? Don't just sit on that nail and do nothing, letting life pass you by. You have the same opportunities as others so get off the nail and do something.

"There are two primary choices in life: to accept conditions as they exist, or accept the responsibility for changing them." Denis Waitley

Taking full responsibility for your life means giving up all your excuses of why you can't or haven't done something. Excuses are our way of not dealing with issues we really should address. We make excuses instead of taking action to change ourselves and then we wonder why we're so unhappy. Sure, we may encounter a busy schedule, a negative spouse, a critical boss, a bad economy, or unsupportive friends and family, but if you allow these to be your crutch for not creating a more fulfilling life for yourself, you will always be held back.

Most people place the blame for everything that isn't the way they want it on outside circumstances, finding an excuse for everything. Blame is a waste of time. Regardless of how much you blame someone or something, it will not change you. When we place the blame for why things aren't going the way we want onto someone or something else, we aren't taking full responsibility. Blaming others is one of the biggest ways we avoid taking responsibility, and it keeps us trapped in a lifestyle we dislike.

Each of us has to create our own joy because no one else can do it for us. If you are waiting for your spouse, boss, parents, friends, or co-workers to change so you can find more enjoyment and fulfillment, be prepared to wait a really long time. If you're not happy with something, it's up to you to do something about it. The happiest women know that to get the most out of life, they must give up blaming and complaining, stop making excuses, and start taking 100% responsibility for creating the kind of life they want.

"People who consider themselves victims of their circumstances will always remain victims unless they develop a greater vision for their lives." Stedman Graham

Make the decision to stop complaining about your life and start living it instead! Here's the plain truth (whether you like to hear it or not): *you have two choices—accept the situation you are at and stop complaining about it, or start taking the steps necessary to create your life the way you want it.* If you find yourself in a situation you don't like, do something to change it. It's up to you to create your future. Start brewing up the life you've always imagined. Happy women take the steps to create the life they want. They don't blame other people for their circumstances. Remember, you are in control of your brew. You hold the pot to your own life in your hands. Only you can change your life; no one else can do it for you.

Grounds for Thought: Are you taking full responsibility for how your life has turned out? What excuses are you clinging to for not making the changes you want? Is there someone or something you've been blaming for the current circumstances in your life? In what areas do you need to start taking more responsibility?

Grounds for Action: When you find yourself complaining about your circumstances, ask yourself if you have taken full responsibility. Then say out loud, *"I will do my part. I will take responsibility."* Either take initiative to change your situation, or quit complaining about it.

JAVA JOLT #2:
Assess the Warmth of Your Current Brew

"Most people struggle with life balance simply because they haven't paid the price to decide what is really important to them." Stephen Covey

When is the last time you stopped to take an inventory of your life and how much you're actually enjoying it? For many women, our one priority is to just make it through each day. We rarely stop long enough to consider if how we are currently living is in alignment with how we want to be living—if our life is giving us joy, fulfillment, and a clear sense of accomplishment. Instead, we put ourselves on autopilot and go through life without ever checking in with ourselves. In order to fully take control of your brew, however, you need to learn how to regularly assess the warmth of your current brew so you can see what areas you need to add a warm-up.

If you are going to create a better, more fulfilling future, you need to first take a truthful look at how satisfied you are with your life as it is today. You can't improve your life without knowing where you're starting from. Are you happy? Are you balanced? What's working? What's not? What areas do you want to improve? Are there areas you've been neglecting? It's time to give yourself a reality check. I have a great tool to help you do just that. It's called Your Pot of Life assessment.

You are one woman with one Pot of Life. This pot holds within it your Life Brew (your time, energy, and attention) which is used to fill the eight essential cups of your life—*relationships, career/life work, physical, financial, personal growth/goals, fun/recreation, spiritual, and helping others.* Each one of these eight areas of life is competing for a bit of your brew. You only have a limited amount of brew, so it's up to you to decide which areas you will pour yourself out to. Since the pot is in your hands, you get to control how much of your brew is poured out into each cup. But, like with any pot of coffee, if you pour too much out into certain cups, there will not be enough in the pot to fill the others. If you fill your life with too much of one area, the others start to become emptied, and you begin to feel unfulfilled and unbalanced.

Your Pot of Life

Relationships Physical Life Brew Personal Growth Spiritual

Career/Life Work Financial Recreation/ Fun Helping Others

I encourage you to honestly evaluate your life with this simple but powerful tool. Rate yourself by shading in each cup the degree to which you are reaching success and satisfaction in that category. A full cup means you feel great in that area (needs no improvement); an empty cup means you feel unsatisfied (needs a lot of improvement). If you'd like a more in-depth exercise to help you break down how fully you are achieving success in each area, you can download a free copy of the full Pot of Life and Life Cups assessment tool at www.theinspirationalcoffeeclub.com.

Consider the following as you are evaluating the key areas of your life:

Relationships: Do you have satisfying, fulfilling relationships with your spouse, kids, parents, and siblings? Do you have great friendships? Are you surrounded by a nurturing, encouraging environment?

Career/Life Work: Are you passionate about your career (whether you're an up-and-coming executive or a stay-at-home mom), are you doing what you want to do in life, do you feel challenged by your work, are you performing at your highest level at your job?

Physical: Are you satisfied with your appearance, look your best, maintain a healthy diet, participate in regular exercise? Do you have any unhealthy addictions? Do you have enough energy to do what you need to each day?

Financial: Are you satisfied with your current income level, have good credit, budget, and save your money wisely? Do you have enough money to do what you want and provide for your family?

Personal Growth: Are you continually growing and learning more about yourself, trying to become a better woman each day? Do you feel happy, whole, and complete? Do you take enough time for yourself? Do you feel like you are clear on your life's purpose and your passions?

Recreation/Fun: Do you have enough fun? Do you regularly take time to enjoy yourself, take vacations or getaways? Do you laugh everyday and take time to enjoy simple pleasures?

Spiritual: Are you actively growing spiritually, expanding your faith, and praying regularly? Do you practice forgiveness, live with gratitude, and love those around you unconditionally?

Helping Others: Do you contribute time to others, or donate time or money to support causes you care about? Do you feel like you make a difference?

Do you feel like you're successful in the areas that matter most to you? Are you pouring the majority of your time and energy into the things that are most important? What areas of your life have you settled for less than you deserve? Are there any areas that you've left completely emptied? I challenge you to honestly evaluate your life and figure out which of these cups is full and which ones you are leaving empty. We all have areas we want to improve so don't feel like you are alone!

Most people are afraid to take a good look at their lives because they are scared they may not like what they see. We often see people who have become successful in one area of life-maybe career or finances-but have completely emptied themselves of another area. When this happens, we become unhappy, unfulfilled, and sometimes even depressed. When you focus on succeeding on only one or two areas of life, you create an imbalance with the other areas. Yet without taking time to stop and evaluate, we don't even realize how unbalanced we are.

Don't expect all your fulfillment, value, and meaning to come from one cup, whether that is work, relationships, or social. If you are focusing too much time on one area of your life, you are limiting success in other areas. You should be distributing some brew into each of your key Life Cups or you'll find your life will cool very quickly.

Remember, your Pot of Life is in your hands. You determine how much of your brew gets poured into each cup. When you identify those areas that are empting you, you can allow yourself to take the necessary steps to spend more time on the things that matter. You have control over how you spend your time and live your life. Be sure you are spending your precious time on the things that truly matter to *you*. No one wants to have a fabulous career but be rejected by family and friends. You cannot justify success in one area at the expense of another. You need to learn how to fill each area.

Of course, some cups will be more filled than others, but none should be empty. Each area plays a critical role in your life happiness. They are all integrally connected. Making regular deposits in each area will enhance your happiness and success. What's most important is to understand this emptying and filling process and learn to recognize those things that are draining you and throwing your life out of balance. By being aware of this, you gain more control over your life.

Focus on getting clear on where your time, energy, and attention go. Become conscious about which cups you're filling and which you are leaving completely empty—which areas you are fulfilled and which ones you are unsatisfied. By doing so you can start to reassess where you pour your time, energy and attention so you can start to live more fully. It's only when you've taken time to assess the warmth of your current brew that you can begin to take steps toward becoming the woman you really want to be. True fulfillment in life cannot happen until you get clear about how you've been living.

"Life without balance can cost you your relationships. Life without balance can cost you your health. Life without balance can cost you your spirituality. Life without balance can cost you your wealth and your happiness. So find things to motivate you from all areas of life. Your success depends on it." Jim Rohn

Grounds for Thought: If nothing changed in your life over the next five years, would you be ok with that? How closely does your present life match the life you want to be living? Are there areas of your life you could be doing better? What can you do to bring greater balance into your life? Do you feel any of your priorities are out of line?

Grounds for Action: Use the Pot of Life diagram to stop and take stock of your current life. Be honest with yourself on how satisfied you currently are in all areas of your life. Which areas are you feeling fulfilled? What areas are you dissatisfied with? For a more in depth review of how fully you are living each area, download a free copy of the Pot of Life and Life Cups assessment at: www.theinspirationalcoffeeclub.com.

JAVA JOLT #3:
Brew Up a Fresh Outlook on Your Future

"The indispensable first step to getting the things you want out of life is this: decide what you want." Ben Stein

The wonderful thing about life is if you don't like what you currently see, you can always change it. You wake up each morning with a refilled, full Pot of Life. You're given another 24 hours to choose how to spend your time, energy, and attention. Once you've taken a good, honest look at how satisfied you are with your current brew, it's time to decide where you'd like to go from here. That means it's time to brew up a fresh outlook on your future and decide how you really want it to look.

So what do you want? For most of us, it's been so long since someone's asked us that. But worse, it's been way too long since we've asked ourselves that question. We spend so much time complaining about the areas we're unsatisfied and unhappy with, but then when asked, '*What would make you happy?*,' the sad fact is that most women don't even know. It's so much easier to point out what we don't like about our lives than to have to take the time and energy to decide how we'd like it to look. But the truth is, if you don't know what you want, you're not going to end up where you want to be. Instead, three, five, or ten years will go by and you'll still be complaining about the same things you are now. Where will you be in 10 years if you continue on the path you're on today?

One of the main reasons women get themselves stuck in a rut is because they have no clear plans for their future. You cannot expect to live your best, most fulfilling life when you live aimlessly. If you want to go somewhere other than where you are right now, you're going to have to start getting your goals organized before you can expect to get anywhere. So how do you do that, you ask. Let me give you some suggestions to help you take control of your future and your happiness and help move you closer to where you want to be.

First, ask yourself this question: *For my cups to be completely full in each area, what would my life look like?* What do you believe would make your life better? What are your hopes and desires for each area? Or, think of it this way—what are you no longer willing to settle for? Make a list of the changes you'd need to make in *each* area in order to feel completely whole, filled, and satisfied. There are always ways to make small changes in the key areas of your life that can dramatically affect your happiness. Redesign your life how you would like to see it. Get clear on what success in these areas means to you. This is how you start to create a vision for your future that excites you. You have so many possibilities in front of you!

Next, since you only have a limited amount of time and energy each day, you are going to need to get your priorities straight and decide which of these areas is most important to you. Don't expect each cup to be completely full (trying to do so could easily burn you out). Keep in mind, some cups will be a lot more important to you than others and that you need to fill those a bit fuller with your time and attention. Ignore trying to be equally balanced in all areas and strive for fullness instead. Figure out *your* priorities and make sure those are getting adequate brew. Pour your time into those areas that genuinely fill you up. Allocate as much time as possible to those areas and activities that are related to what you feel is truly worthwhile. There's a big difference between being busy and really accomplishing something worthwhile. In order to have true satisfaction, you must make sure you are spending your time on things that matter most to you so you can focus your time, energy, and attention on pursuing goals that will enhance those areas.

Which of the eight key life areas are most important to you? Relationships, spiritual, physical health, financial, personal growth, career, helping others, fun? To help you, go back to Your Pot of Life and Life Cups assessment above and label each cup #1 to #8 in order of importance to you (#1 being most important; #8 being least important). What do you have to do differently to make sure you're putting enough energy into the areas you value most? What goals do you want to set for yourself in those areas? More time with your family? More fulfilling job? Healthier weight or lifestyle? More money in your savings? More time studying the Bible? Learning a new hobby? Taking a vacation? Get clear on your priorities. And line up your life with what really matters to you.

Only you can define your priorities. Figure out what areas matter most to you and treat them as such. When you identify the things that matter most to you, it's easier to determine how to split your time. As women we've been taught that we can have it all. But trying to have it all at the exact same time is overwhelming. You end up feeling frazzled, burned out, and defeated in so many other areas. Pour your time, energy, and attention into those areas that matter most and your life will be much richer for it.

Consider which areas you believe would make the most difference in your happiness and enjoyment level right now. If you're like most women, you have changes that you'd like to make in every area. But you can't change every area at once or you'll get overwhelmed and frustrated, so start with those areas that are most important to you. You've got to identify what areas of your life you most want to improve. You do this by looking at those Life Cups and determining which of those eight areas of your life needs the most improvement (don't feel bad—there isn't a single one of us who doesn't need improvement). Consider which improvements would make the most significant difference in your life.

The final and probably most important insight for taking control of your future is to be truthful about what *you* want. We spend so much time pursuing things we think others want for us. Now it's time for you—not your parent's or spouse's or boss's goals for you. Stop comparing yourself to others or setting goals for your future that you think others want for you. Your life goals have to be right for you in order to keep you excited about working toward them. We are all at a different stage of our lives in our careers, finances, relationships, health, etc. You must do what feels best in your heart. Make your life more like yours. Don't structure your brew to be like those around you. Find your own balance that fulfills and satisfies you. Incidentally, do you know what it's called when you try to steal someone else's version of their life cups? *A mugging!* Do not get accused of mugging someone else's life. Don't live someone else's vision. Live yours. Your best friend might pour her heart into her career, where you pour your heart into your family. There's nothing wrong with that. What's best for others is not necessarily what's best for you. As long as you are doing what makes you happy, your cup is full. Your cups should not look just like your sister's, girlfriend's, boss's, etc. Only you can define what success, happiness, and balance means to you. Society, your family, and your friends will all try to tell you what success should look like, but when you decide for yourself and stick to it, you'll experience more joy than you ever imagined. Get clear on what you want out of life.

We always need to keep fresh goals for our life in front of us. We need to continue to add freshness or our brew will get cold and we'll lose our enthusiasm for life. Your life can grow stagnant in any area. When we stop making deposits in each area, our life grows cold. If we're not growing, we're not living. Your life goals change as your life changes, so be sure to touch base regularly with yourself to make sure you're not living off an old brew.

I encourage you to make the decision that you will do whatever you need to create the kind of future you desire for your life. What needs to happen for your cups to be filled? Only about eight percent of the general population can identify clear goals for their life and only three percent ever actually write those down. Having your Pot of Life and Life Cups defined will separate you from most everyone else. Refuse to leave your future in someone else's hands. Decide what you want out of your life and go for it!

"It's never too late to become the person you might have been." George Elliot

Grounds for Thought: What's next for you? Are you clear about how you want your life to look five-ten years from now? Do you know what success looks and feels like to you? Have you written a plan for your life yet? Do you have any goals for yourself? What are the three most significant areas you would like to change? Will you leave the next five years up to chance or will you start taking more control of your future?

Grounds for Action: Take time now before you move onto the next chapter to make a list of goals you want to accomplish. It's time to create a vision for your life that excites YOU—to find the right balance and right goals for you and your life. What would your life look like if you could have it the way you want it? Get clear on what you really want in each of the key areas of your life. Then, clarify what matters most to you and design a recipe for change. How would you like your cups to look one year from now? Five years from now?

Being able to visualize your goals and your future is a key step in making them happen. Cut out pictures that represent your goals for the future and words that inspire you to move forward. This will keep you motivated while pursuing them. I've taken an empty coffee canister, decorated it with flowers and quotes on the outside and placed all the pictures, words and phrases that describe my future inside of it. Keep track of your life's journey with your personalized coffee canister. Or, if you aren't a coffee drinker, create a dream board with all your goals or paste them in your journal. Start working toward making those goals a reality so you can have the future *you* desire!

"Tell me, what is it you plan to do with your one wild and precious life?" Mary Oliver

JAVA JOLT #4:
Don't Forget to Press the 'ON' Button!

"Even if you're on the right track, you'll get run over if you just sit there." Will Rogers

The final and most essential step toward taking control of your brew is to remember to press the 'ON' button! I think this is the piece that limits many of us. We have great plans and goals for the future, but then forget to put any action behind them. Just dreaming and planning your future won't create it. Remember, action and motivation needs to come from you. If you really want things to change in any area of your life, you are going to need to be the one who puts the time and energy into making that change happen. No one else is going to do it for you. Think of it this way: if you want to get in shape, you can't hire a personal trainer to do the workouts for you; you have to put the time and energy into doing them yourself or else nothing will change in your life. If you want to change your life, *you* are going to have to do it.

Non-action is the biggest waste of our abilities and time. The difference between those who spend their lives dreaming and those who spend their lives achieving, is that one has learned to stop dreaming and to start doing. Some push the 'ON' button themselves while others wait for someone else to come push it for them. Are you doing anything to make your life better or are you just wishing things were different?

**Second Cup Story:**

A story is told of a woman in desperate need of changing her financial situation so she goes to church to ask God for help. *"Dear Lord,"* she prays, *"If I don't get some cash, I'm going to lose everything. Please let me win the lottery."* Lottery night comes, but she doesn't win.

The next week she prays even harder, saying, *"God, I'm counting on you. I need your help. Please just let me win this once."* Lottery night comes again and no luck. A week later and still no richer, the woman prays one more time, saying, *"God, I don't seem to be getting through to you. I've been really good. Give me a break. Let me win the lottery."*

Suddenly the heavens open up, there is a blinding flash of light, and a deep voice says, *"Give me a break, lady! Buy a ticket!"*

We can't just define our ideal vision for our lives and expect we'll get there. Identifying changes you'd like to make in your life doesn't do you any good if you aren't actively doing your part to make them happen. Stop crossing your fingers and hoping things will change. You need to be the one who does it.

The world is full of people who have good intentions. Dreams they'd like to pursue, goals they'd like to achieve, and changes they'd like to make. But there is something more important than good intentions and that is action. There are many dreamers out there, but there aren't enough who will move ahead and take the steps necessary to achieve the life they desire. You will change nothing in your life with good intentions. Intentions are useless. We have a good intention to do something and then before you know it a year passes and nothing has changed. That year turns into five years then ten years. The intent was there, but nothing happened. Intention without action is useless.

Start doing something to make your life more enjoyable. Make sure you are moving forward, not standing still. Make it a goal to get just a little bit better each day. What matters most is that you step up to life, even when you least feel like it. For those of you who are saying to yourself, *"I just don't feel motivated,"* you have it backward. You need to do something first before you begin to feel any motivation. Motivation follows the action. Motivation creates energy. Energy comes after you take the first steps. So stop waiting to 'feel' like doing something and just do it.

Ask yourself what one or two small things you can do today to start moving yourself forward. Take baby steps, and you'll be amazed over time how much distance you can cover. Take, for instance, this book. It's been a work in progress for nearly two years. Sometimes I felt like quitting—that it would never be done! But every day I'd make it a goal to work on it, even if just for 10-20 minutes sometimes. The small increments add up. When you add together your efforts, look what you have—a beautiful accomplishment! If there's a goal you have that feels out of reach, I encourage you to not give up. Make daily step-by-step progress, and eventually you will reach your destination.

Remember, life changes take time. They're long-term efforts which start with small, daily steps. You cannot write a book overnight, you cannot lose thirty pounds in two weeks, you cannot run a marathon in a week, and you cannot pay off large debts in a month. All these things take time, energy, effort, and perseverance. Our society is one of instant gratification, but we have to remember that we need to be patient and not give up when things are taking longer than we hoped they would. (Things almost always take longer than you think they should.) But when you finally reach that goal—which you will—the sense of pride and accomplishment is like none other! Just as instant coffee isn't nearly as tasty as the slower-brewed kind, same is true of the things we want most in life. Taking control of your brew means being willing to put in the time to create your ideal life, regardless of how long it takes you to get there.

Life changes aren't always easy. It takes commitment and discipline. Taking control of your brew means doing whatever is necessary to create the kind of future you desire. If you need support and accountability in making life changes, learn more about personal coaching programs at www.theinspirationalcoffeeclub.com.

Grounds for Thought: Have you pressed the 'ON' button for your life or are you waiting for someone else to come do it for you? Are you willing to actively do your part to make your best life a reality? What steps do you need to start taking today to live the kind of life you desire?

Grounds for Action: Pick one area of your life you'd like to work on and identify a goal you want to achieve in that area (short or long-term goal). Write out a step-by-step plan for achieving it, and then start doing one small thing each day toward your goal. Identify the first step you need to take and decide when you will take it. You can, day-by-day, begin to alter the course of your future. Change happens slowly, but if you are persistent, you will end up where you want to be.

The Last Cup

Taking control of your brew sounds like one of the most basic strategies, but it's truly one of the most difficult to implement. It takes discipline and willingness to take action. The plain truth is that you cannot improve your life without action on your part. There are many people who are living what I call the lukewarm life—a place where they're not really happy, but they're not unhappy enough to do anything about it. That's a dangerous place. It's a place where we numb ourselves to our true desires and accept what's in front of us instead of progressing toward what we really want in life. Refuse to live a lukewarm life. It's up to you to create the kind of life that makes you happy.

I know it's easy to feel like you're going backwards. Maybe you're not where you wanted to be, your checkbook used to be fuller, your pants used to be looser, or you used to be able to walk a mile without being out of breath. Remember, the secret to success is to look ahead—not back! Live the life that's in front of you, not the one that's past. There's no point in looking back at all the things you haven't done. Instead, acknowledge where you are and where you want to be then determine what it will take to get yourself there.

Your life still has bottomless possibilities. Remember, you are not stuck in a place you cannot escape. If your life has become stale, take a fresh look at yourself, define where you want to be, and develop a plan of action for getting there. Make the decision today that you are going to love your life. Remember, it's the only one you've got. Don't settle for a life that is not fulfilling and satisfying. Realize you deserve more. Be determined and refuse to give up on the life you want in any area. Those who live life to the fullest make the decision not to give up or let someone else control their happiness.

If you want to know where you are going to be five years from now, you need to start planning it now. Remember, it's your responsibility to create what you want to experience in the next years of your life. You have more control over your life than you think you do. It's your life— brew it the way you want to see it. I've made the decision to take control of my future. Have you?

"The greatest thing in the world is not so much where we are, but in what direction we are moving." Oliver Wendell Holmes

GROUND RULE #5

Don't Be Afraid to Burn Your Tongue ~ Take Some Chances

"Unless you try to do something beyond what you have already mastered, you will never grow." Ronald E. Osborn

Unless You Like a Cold, Bland Life, You're Going to Have to Risk a Burn!

"We cannot become what we need to be by remaining what we are." Max DePree

When is the last time you did something beyond your normal comfort zone? Ironically, most of us desire to try new things, but at the same time we resist change. For the majority of us, we go through life never wanting to feel uncomfortable, but by doing this, we short change ourselves. The only way to avoid new things is to stay trapped where we are, but there is little growth or enjoyment in that. New experiences are where the joy lies. Part of truly savoring life is developing a positive attitude toward new opportunities. You've got to get out there and take some chances. Those who have a true fullness for life realize the importance of trying new things and living outside their comfort zone—they aren't afraid to burn their tongue a time or two. Unless you like drinking a cold, bland life, you're going to have to risk a burn to truly taste the richness life offers.

Burning your tongue means enjoying new experiences that stretch you. People often cling to what they know, even if they aren't satisfied with it. People would rather stay and complain than try something different and risk failing. If you want to grow as a woman, you must continue to push yourself to do things you've never done. You can't become who you really want to be by remaining the same.

We have a strong tendency to fear or be nervous about new experiences. We tell ourselves, *"I'm ready for a change!"* or *"I'm tired of the same old thing!"* and then we hesitate to embrace the new things when they come. Instead, we resist, shrink back in fear, and restore ourselves to our normal comfort zones. I still struggle with this each time I get my hair highlighted. I tell myself, *"This will be the time I try a new color."* And I wrestle for weeks if I should do red highlights, dark highlights, or lighter highlights. I look through pictures in magazines and the Internet telling myself I will try something new. Then, the day I get to the salon and my stylist asks, *"What are we going to do today?"* I immediately say, *"Let's do the same as last time!"* Can any of you relate?

"All life is a chance. So take it! The person who goes furthest is the one who is willing to do and dare." Dale Carnegie

Women tend to be more uncomfortable with risk and change than men are. We worry far more about making mistakes or making a wrong choice so we second guess our decisions and often remain crippled by indecisiveness. We want to stay with something familiar so we're more scared to move on and experience new things. We are creatures of habit, and it is so easy to get into a rut. Without venturing into the unknown, however, you'll never experience life as it could be. If you don't try new things, you are missing so many new and wonderful experiences.

Life will ask us to do things that seem scary. We fear applying for a new job in case we don't get it, we fear starting a new relationship because it may not work out, we fear living our dreams because there's the chance we could fail, we fear starting a new diet because it might not work, we fear a new hairstyle because we may end up liking our old one better. But what happens to those who are so afraid to live and take some chances? You won't get any of the rewards you so desire. You need to overcome your fear of living and learn to live more boldly. Don't let fear rule your life with things that may or may not happen.

I heard a wonderful phrase once that has stuck with me for years: *"You don't risk stubbing your toe by standing still, but you also don't get anywhere!"* It's the same way in life. You don't have to risk getting burned if you never try things outside your comfort zone, but you also don't get to experience the richness that life offers. The path of least resistance is usually the most unfulfilling. A key part to living life to the fullest is to start taking more chances.

"Life is either a daring adventure or nothing." Helen Keller

Too many of us are bored with life. It's time to start burning your tongue so you can give your life the refreshing jolt it needs. Stepping even just a little bit out of your comfort zone can make life exciting and full. If you dare to take some chances, you will discover a fulfillment to life that you never realized was there. When you stretch your comfort zone and strive to take risks, you find more opportunities and growth than you ever imagined. Be willing to risk some burns. The following strategies will help you learn how to take more chances and overcome the fear of burning your tongue.

Grounds for Thought: Do you embrace new challenges or are you afraid to take chances? Are you hiding inside your comfort zone? Are you in a rut? When is the last time you took a chance on something? How would you rate your current risk-taking ability? What's holding you back?

JAVA JOLT #1:
Acknowledge the "Grounds" in your Brew

"The greatest mistake you can make in life is to be continually fearing you will make one." Elbert Hubbard

Though we may not recognize its power over us, most of us let fear hold us back from living the life we are fully capable of. Fear is the number one reason people hesitate to try anything new. I call your fears the "grounds" that find their way into your brew and threaten to spoil your fulfillment. Oftentimes we fail to see the opportunities in front of us because of our fears that are limiting us. But really, the only limits we have are the ones we put on ourselves. The first step to taking more chances is to acknowledge the fears that are holding you back.

There are all kinds of fears that rob us from trying new things. Fear of failure, fear of rejection, fear of change, fear of disappointment, fear of making wrong choices, fear of the unknown, fear of not being good enough, fear of people disapproving of us, fear of something being too difficult. Any of these sound familiar? Too often we hold ourselves back from the things we'd really like to try, out of a fear of looking foolish, feeling stupid, or making a mistake. If you spend your time worrying about everything that can go wrong, you basically can talk yourself out of anything. And if you play it safe, you risk something even greater—the opportunity to experience the joy that comes from pursuing the things you really want. And even worse, you're left with a haunting inner voice that will forever say, *'what if?'*

If you want to live a more fulfilling life, then you have to get a grip on your fears. You cannot allow fear to paralyze you. People who are ruled by fear stay where it's safe, and there's danger in that because we can't reach our true potential by staying where it's safe. Fear makes us afraid of doing something that might be beneficial to us. Living outside our comfort zone will require us to move into the unknown and that can be scary. We cling to what we *do* know and fear what we *don't* know. But if we cave into our fears, we don't grow. We short-change ourselves by choosing to keep things the way they are instead of the way we really would like them to be. Ironically, studies show that 95 percent of what we fear is unjustified.

There used to be a time when we weren't ruled by fear of new things. Think of the day you got on a bike for the first time. When you fell, you most likely got right back up and tried again. Over and over and over. There was a time when you felt like nothing was unattainable for you. Then, as time went by, fear reared its ugly mug in your life. And now many of us go through life not wanting to try anything new for fear that we might fail. Whether we are 20 or 60, many of us become so scared of trying and failing that we don't go after what we truly want. We play it safe and hold on so tight to the status quo that we never experience what could be. Don't be so afraid of burning your tongue that you miss out on many great opportunities.

It's important that you understand that *everyone* has fears. There is not a single person who is immune to them. So you can gain comfort knowing you are not the only one feeling it. You may look at others who are taking chances and taking risks and think they are so brave because they aren't afraid to put themselves out there. On the contrary! They had to overcome a lot of fears to get where they are at today, but they're still pushing forward. Don't let your mind feed you the illusion that others are special, different, have less fear, or have it easier than you. Perhaps you've heard of this famous lady.

Second Cup Story:

Today, Paula Dean is the well-known 'Queen of Southern Cooking' author and food entrepreneur on the Food Network. She seems so confident and extroverted, but did you know that she suffered from severe agoraphobia—fear of leaving her home—for over two decades?

For 20 years, she focused only on cooking for her family because it was something she could do without leaving her home and venturing outside her comfort zone. It wasn't until she and her first husband divorced and at 43-years old was forced to provide for herself and her sons that she pushed beyond her fears. She forced herself to. And now look where she is today because she conquered her fears and moved forward. Trust me, there isn't a single person immune to fear.

I used to think that confident women were the lucky ones who didn't feel fear. Actually, I've learned that confident women feel fear, too. In fact, they probably feel more fear than most because they put themselves in situations outside their comfort zones more often. But the key is confident women feel the fear and do it anyway! They accept that it's the price they have to pay for progress. As long as you continue to grow, you are going to feel fear. In fact, if you haven't felt fear recently, that's a good indication you aren't taking enough chances. If you are the type who will do anything to avoid the uncomfortable feeling of fear, you run the bigger risk of never getting what you want in life. When fear rears its ugly mug (and it will), just remind yourself that no one ever died from disappointment, rejection, or failure.

The fear of failure is one of the biggest hurdles people have to confront if they intend to live life to the fullest. Most of us are so afraid of failing that it keeps us from even trying. Your fears have created a comfort zone that is actually limiting your happiness and success. We try to stay safe, but that keeps us from growing, from using our fullest potential, and from living life to the very fullest! We were created to try new things and take some chances.

It takes guts to acknowledge your fears and realize they are holding you back. These "grounds" you are carrying around with you are preventing you from tasting all that life has to offer. Only when you acknowledge and conquer your fears, can you fully live your best life. Don't let fear keep you from taking action and making the necessary changes that will give you the life you desire. On the other side of your fear is something beneficial awaiting you. Your ability to confront your fears is one of the most important keys to living a fulfilling life. Don't let fear slow you down! Look fear straight in the eye and move forward toward the life you want.

Grounds for Thought: How many times have you tried to do something new and resisted? In what ways have you let fear hold you back from doing something you really wanted to do? What are you afraid will happen if you move forward? What fears and self-doubts surface just as you are about to try something new?

Grounds for Action: On a coffee filter (or any sheet of paper for you non-coffee drinkers), make a list of the fears and hesitations that hold you back from trying new things (fear of failing, looking stupid, not being good enough, rejection, not being liked, not being smart enough, not being attractive enough, etc.) You can't overcome your fears unless you first recognize they exist. Then crumple it up and throw it away (feel free to step on it a few times so that you can feel like you're stomping your fears). While you do this say, *"I will not let fear hold me back."*

JAVA JOLT #2:
Filter Your Fears and Replace Them with Faith and Courage

"The only things that stand between a person and what they want in life are the will to try it, and the faith to believe it's possible." Rich Devos

If you are looking for advice on making your fears magically go away, then I'm going to burst your bubble. It doesn't work that way. If you're waiting for all the fear to go away before you start taking some chances then you'll be waiting your whole life. The only way to get rid of the fear of doing something is to go out and do the very thing we fear doing. Doing it actually comes before the fear goes away. No matter how much we wish we could just make our fears go away, we can't escape them, but we can learn to filter them so they do not have to keep us stuck. Unfortunately, most of us forget to put this filter in and we allow our fears to stop us from moving forward. If you want to learn how to take more chances, you are going to have to start filtering out the doubts and fears that hold you back and replace them with something even more powerful—a blend of faith and courage.

Fear is the most powerful of all thoughts with one exception—faith. Only faith can help you overcome fear, so learn to start filtering out all the fears and start filling your mind with a healthy dose of faith. Faith is the willingness to take risks and overcome your fears even when the outcome is uncertain. It's trusting that everything will work out as it's supposed to. At some point, you need to be willing to say, sink or swim, I'm going to go after my dreams, do what I want to do, move forward, and try something new. Take your first sips in faith. If it doesn't work, you can always do something else. Take this attitude with you: try something new and if it doesn't work out, so what. You tried. You need to stop focusing only on what might go wrong and start focusing more on what might go right. When you do this, you let your faith be greater than your fear.

True, you may try something and it may not work out. Acting in faith means that you accept that sometimes God's answer is a 'no.' And when something doesn't work out, it's God's way of telling you that you're moving in the wrong direction. He can use your failures to nudge you in a different direction. But if you never took the chance and stepped out in faith, how would you ever know? Hold a firm belief that whatever happens will be for your own good, guiding you one step closer to where you are meant to be.

Maybe you started a new business that didn't work out. Or pursued a relationship that failed. Of course it burns! But that experience will take you down a whole new path. There will always be something else that comes, you just have to keep looking and keep the faith. Trust God with the results of your life. You don't need to fear burns. God has a plan for your life. No one knows what's past the next burn. Don't spend so much time focused on that last burn that you fail to see the next opportunity in front of you.

Having the courage to trust that you can handle anything that happens is much more important than whether or not you succeed. And faith only grows when we take action *without* knowing the end result. God tells us we need to walk by faith and not by sight. Think about this: everything you know was once unknown to you. Did you always know how to do your job? How to be a parent? How you'd like that new hairstyle? How to ride a bike? How you'd be able to adjust moving to a new city? They all require you to do something outside your comfort zone. Taking action in spite of your fears helps you develop the faith and courage you need.

"Take the first step in faith. You don't have to see the whole staircase, just take the first step." Martin Luther King Jr.

I think of my own self in starting The Inspirational Coffee Club. For years, I had this idea in my head and a burning desire to start my own business, but I kept saying to myself, *"When I'm not so afraid, then I'll go for it."* I kept thinking, that somehow, if I just kept waiting, my fears would subside and I'd feel more confident in pursuing this dream of mine. But the fears never went away. In fact, as I started to take small steps toward this dream, the fears got more real, but I learned to recognize them as "grounds" that were attempting to suppress my dream. The only thing that allowed me to push past those fears was my faith to trust that it would work out as it's meant to be and the courage to believe I could handle anything that happened to me. And I've learned that most of us have far more courage than we realize.

"You can never cross the ocean unless you have the courage to lose sight of the shore." Christopher Columbus

I'm convinced it takes a large dose of faith and courage to be happy—to pursue the desires within, to apply for that new job, to leave that bad relationship, to start that new diet or new aerobics class, to purchase that new house, to speak in front of that group, to compete in that race, to go back to school, to pursue a whole new career direction, to take on that new volunteer position, to start dating again at middle-age. As long as you continue to stretch your abilities, to take new risks to live the life you want to live and to try new things, you are going to experience fear. But if you go through life too afraid of failure, you will never fully live.

Consider it a relief that now you no longer have to work so hard on getting rid of your fear. It isn't going to go away. Instead, you need to learn to acknowledge your fears, filter them out, and develop a strong blend of courage and faith. When you attempt to try something new and those ugly fears rise to the top again, remember to take the first sips in faith. When you learn to push forward in spite of your fears, fear loses its grip on you. Courage and faith can give you victory over your fears. Always remember; it sometimes takes a leap of faith in order to soar.

"Courage doesn't always roar. Sometimes courage is the little voice at the end of the day that says I'll try again tomorrow." Mary Anne Radmacher

Grounds for Thought: Is there an area of your life in which you need to step forward in faith? Have you ever found that fear sometimes overpowers your faith? Do you believe you have the courage to handle whatever happens? Think about times you took a risk and won.

Grounds for Action: Grab a clean sheet of paper or coffee filter and in large letters write 'FAITH' and 'COURAGE.' In smaller writing, make a list of experiences in which you stepped out in faith, not knowing the final outcome at the time. Tape that to the fridge or the wall and look at it often. Continue to add to that list as you step out more and more in faith to live fully. Each time you attempt something outside your comfort zone, say a prayer and ask to be led in the right direction. Then remind yourself whatever happens, you can handle it. Every time I start to feel uncomfortable outside my comfort zone, I say to myself, *"My faith is bigger than my fear."*

JAVA JOLT #3:
Start Burning and Learning

"There are no secrets to success. It is the result of preparation, hard work, and learning from failure." Colin Powell

I already know what you are thinking right now. *"Yeah, but what if I try and fail?"* or *"What if I take a chance and things don't turn out?"* You know what, that might very well be the case and if so, good for you! That means you've had what I call a "Burn and Learn" experience. You've learned what not to do again next time. If at first you don't succeed, then join the club. You're in good company! Life is not about never failing. It's about picking yourself up when you fall. Learn from the burns but don't let the possibility of failing keep you from moving forward in life.

You need to change the way you look at failure because failures and mistakes can prove to be very valuable. Don't look at these experiences as failing; look at them as "Burn and Learn" experiences.

You may stumble and fall a bit through life, but you need to get yourself up, brush off, and try again. Quit being so fearful that you're too afraid to try anything new. The most fulfilled women realize that making mistakes is part of living. They confidently seek out and accept new opportunities for growth. Then they learn from their mistakes and grow from their failures. You've got to make mistakes to get closer to where you want to be. Don't let rejection keep you down. When you get burned, don't lose the lesson. No failure is permanent. A burn is just a temporary setback in a fulfilling life.

It's not always easy. Burns can hurt, sting and leave an uncomfortable feeling for quite awhile. But never stop drinking in new life experiences. Taking new chances keeps life interesting. Yes, you may burn your tongue, but a burn shouldn't stop you. Burns heal. Plus, they are a reminder of chances taken and opportunities pursued. There's something admirable to be said about that. When's the last time you failed at something?

What really helped me overcome my fear of failure was realizing that it can be a great teacher and motivator. One of my favorite concepts is this idea of "Burning and Learning." It means getting started, making some mistakes, correcting them, and moving forward. Through each failure, we learn lessons that will reduce our risk of failing in the future and increase our chances for even greater fulfillment and success. Mistakes are just opportunities for learning something new.

If you attempt to take action and fail in your attempt, you are most certainly not a failure. In fact, you are a success because you tried. You took a risk and went for it. There is value in that action. When you take big risks, it's not always going to work out. So what? Everything in life involves some sort of risk. Isn't your life worth it?

"Success is 99 percent failure." Soichiro Honda

Our world is full of stories of people who have failed numerous times before they succeeded. Everyone who has ever achieved big dreams has experienced failure and learned to make their failures learning experiences rather than defeats. J.K. Rowling, author of the *'Harry Potter'* series, was rejected by 12 publishers. Oprah Winfrey was fired from her first job as a reporter for empathizing with the people she interviewed. The authors of *'Chicken Soup for the Soul'* were rejected by 140 publishers before it became the empire it is today. See a pattern? The most successful and happy people aren't the ones who have made the least mistakes. They are the ones who have failed numerous times, but kept moving forward.

I have "Burn and Learn" experiences on a weekly basis. Anytime you put yourself out there, you're opening yourself up to more failures, of course. But you're also opening yourself up to so much more opportunity for success. I think of how many times I submit a speaking proposal for a group who instead chooses a different speaker or how many times I've ordered a new product and learned that there are issues with the printing or design. Sure, these things are disappointing, but I don't let them keep me down. Failure isn't failure if you learn from it and do better next time.

"Remember, success is not measured by heights attained but by obstacles overcome. We're going to pass through many obstacles in our lives: good days, bad days. But the successful person will overcome those obstacles and constantly move forward." Bruce Jenner, American Olympian

Your failures and mistakes can become some of your best learning experiences. Early in my speaking career I was asked to do a keynote address for a Women's Expo. For those of you who don't know, public speaking is the #1 fear. I had the same anxiety that most do: *"What if they don't like me?" "I don't know if I can do this."* Well, half-way through the presentation three-fourths of the audience got up and left. I was humiliated and mortified. I instantly thought the women weren't enjoying the talk or didn't like what I was saying. I felt like I had failed. I composed myself and made it through the talk. Afterwards, the event planner came up to me and said, *"I am so sorry. We scheduled the drawing for the big diamond at the same time as your speech and the ladies had to be present to win."* Well, thank goodness it wasn't me! But if I took that same experience and carried it with me into every other speaking engagement I'm asked to do, I'd never speak again. Instead I used this burn as an opportunity to learn these two important lessons: 1). Diamonds, not coffee, are a girl's best friend! 2). Always confirm the schedule of events whenever I'm speaking.

We all make mistakes. Learn from them and use them to make better decisions next time. Honestly, whether you fall down along the way matters very little. Remember the example about riding a bike. Did you just get on and ride right away? No! You tipped over many times. It took time to master. You needed to fall in order to learn. The key is you'd get back on the bike each time and get better and better each day until one day you mastered it. Once you learn it, you learn it. Don't be afraid of failing. Because without some burning, you can't keep learning. Consider the story of Thomas Edison.

 **Second Cup Story:** The 10,000 Step Light Bulb

Did you know that it took Thomas Edison 10,000 tries before he invented the light bulb? During an interview once, a reporter asked him, *"How does it feel to fail 9,999 times?"* To this, Edison replied, *"I didn't fail 9,999 times. The light bulb was an invention of 9,999 steps."*
Just imagine if he had given up after the 9,999th time!

"Many of life's failures are people who did not realize how close they were to success when they gave up." Thomas Edison

Not only is it ok to fail, but it is proof you are improving. Don't see setbacks or rejection as things to avoid; rather, they are marks of a great journey and should be appreciated, even celebrated. Burns just might be the very things that help you break through to a new level of success and happiness in life. If you aren't failing, you aren't getting any better. If you are going to get better, you have to push yourself. If you push yourself, you are going to fail. Never let a week go by without burning your tongue.

"Burn and Learn" experiences are all around us. Every day we're given opportunities to stretch, grow, and experience something wonderful and new. Look for new opportunities to stretch outside your comfort zone in the pursuit of joy. Otherwise, you stay paralyzed in a life of mediocrity. You try that new dessert recipe and it flops. You try that new hairstyle you liked and it doesn't look good on you. You applied for that big promotion and someone else got it. So what if it doesn't work out the first time? Be daring, be adventurous. Don't let fear hold you back. Burn and learn! Trying something new may feel uncomfortable at first, but real growth happens when you move through this discomfort and decide you aren't afraid to burn your tongue. Resist the urge to go back to what's easy.

Get out there and experiment, try out new situations, and push your boundaries once in awhile. Don't worry so much about making mistakes because that's how we learn and grow. If you fail, who cares! When you get knocked down, get right back up and keep trying. Think of it this way: if you step up to the plate, of course you may strike out, but if you never try, you will never know the joy of hitting a home run. Even the best ball players strike out. But people remember their home runs; not their strike outs.

"Progress always involves risks. You can't steal second base and keep your foot on first." Frederick B. Wilcox

Second Cup Story:

Take a lesson from a famous sports star in our society—former NBA standout Michael Jordan. He is quoted saying, *"I have missed over 900 shots, lost over 200 games, and 24 times I was put in to make the game-winning shot and missed. I've failed over and over and over. And that's why I succeed."* He realized that along the road to success he would experience some failure, but didn't let that stop him from leaving his legacy in basketball.

Failure is a healthy, inevitable part of life. If you want more life in you, you've got to start taking some more chances. Try new things, take a risk, and challenge yourself! If it works, wonderful. If it doesn't, then try something else. When one burn occurs, a fresh beginning is just around the corner. Don't stay burned. Get back up. You are never a failure when you look at new experiences as "Burn and Learn" opportunities.

"The men who try to do something and fail are infinitely better than those who try to do nothing and succeed." Lloyd Jones

Grounds for Thought: When was the last time you attempted something that didn't work out? What did you learn from the experience? If you can't remember the last time you took a risk and failed, what does that say about you? What are some things you'd like to do that you've been too afraid to try for fear of failing?

Grounds for Action: Think about one thing you can do each week to step outside your comfort zone or try something new. Be on the lookout for new opportunities: a different hair color or style, a new recipe, an outfit you wouldn't normally wear, a new shade of lipstick, sign up for an art class or cooking class, go to dinner and a movie by yourself, try out for the Community Theater or Church choir, submit your resume for that job you've been contemplating, sign up for a new volunteer opportunity, give that Pilates class a shot, try a new kind of food, give yourself a manicure with a vibrant color you aren't normally accustomed to, take a dance or aerobics class you've never tried (Zumba is getting very popular), learn a new instrument or hobby, paint a room or wall in your home a color you wouldn't normally think of. The ideas are endless to get you out of your comfort zone. Sometimes it's as simple as going to a coffee shop or café alone and enjoying a cup of coffee by yourself. Burn your tongue and see how good it feels after you've stepped beyond your comfort zone.

JAVA JOLT #4:
Set Some "Burn Your Tongue" Dreams for Your Life

"The greater danger for most of us is not that our aim is too high and we miss it, but that it is too low and we reach it." Michelangelo

It's important to think big when it comes to dreams for your future. Sadly, most of us dream such small dreams for our life; we underestimate our own abilities. We don't want to set high goals for ourselves in case those dreams don't come true. We tell ourselves to be careful, to not get our hopes too high. But what good are low hopes? We can do so much more than we think we can. I recommend you think big thoughts, dream big dreams, and make big plans. Set some "burn your tongue" goals for your life that stretch you!

It's so important to have goals for your life that are bigger than where you are right now. Big dreams are what give your life passion and enthusiasm. Think of the time you made it a goal to save for a dream vacation you've wanted to take. Or to work toward that book you've wanted to write. Or train for that race you've always wanted to compete in. Life wakes up when you have big goals. There are a lot of people who have lost their dreams. Are you one of them?

Maybe you dream of getting your Master's degree or PhD, opening a business, writing a cookbook for your family and friends, getting your pilot's license, mastering your computer skills, losing 50 pounds, or taking your children or parents on a vacation. Keep pressing forward. Keep believing in your dreams. Most of us give up too easily. We tell ourselves: *"I didn't get that new job; I'm just meant to stay in this unfulfilling one." "I failed the test; I'm not meant to go to grad school." "I couldn't finish my first race, I'm just not meant to be a runner." "I can't lose this weight, I'm just meant to be unhealthy." "My business failed; I'm not meant to be my own boss."* Don't let a few failures get in the way of continuing to pursue your heart's desires. Take Maxcy Filer for example.

**Second Cup Story:**

At the age of 36, Maxcy Filer, with a wife and two young boys at home, dreamed of becoming an attorney. He was inspired by other attorneys who were making changes in laws that were improving his community and he too wanted to be a part of that change.

So Maxcy went to law school, graduated, and took the bar exam. And like many people, Maxcy failed the bar on his first attempt. So he tried again. And again. And again. Maxcy Filer continued to take the bar exam while his sons graduated from high school. And he continued to take the bar exam even after his two sons had graduated from law school and earned law degrees of their own. And he continued to take the bar exam after he was working for his sons as a law clerk in their offices.

After 25 years and 47 attempts, Maxcy Filer *finally* passed the bar at the age of 61 when most people start thinking about retirement. And today, he's living the dream he's always wanted to live. It just took a little longer than he had planned.

Too often we settle for where we are because we are scared to try something new and fail. Then we give up too easily on our dreams if they don't happen quickly or easily enough. When disappointment or rejection knocks you down, get back up. Don't give up. There's always something better in store. Just because you get burned doesn't mean you should give up. Keep pressing forward. Don't make the mistake of sitting back and settling where you are simply so you don't have to face failure. Set some "burn your tongue" goals for your life. If you achieve them—wonderful! If not, so be it. Don't ever feel small for having attempted something important in your heart and failing. If you've failed pursuing a desire in your heart then I'm proud of you. I hope you are proud of yourself.

If you don't have obstacles to overcome, you probably haven't set goals worth achieving! Life can be easy but unfulfilling. A lot of people believe there shouldn't be any obstacles. There will always be obstacles however. You just have to deal with them. No obstacles means no progress. If you don't have some obstacles, you are not playing a big enough game. Set bigger goals for yourself. Bring your fears to the surface, filter them out, and go for it! The only failure is the failure to try.

"You'll always miss 100% of the shots you don't take." Wayne Gretsky

I've learned how fun it is to have big dreams. A few months ago, I took my computer to a local coffee shop to write while enjoying a cup of coffee. Before I knew it, I was looking at their shelves of products and found myself daydreaming about how they could rearrange their shelves to make room for my products. And this was a national chain of coffee shops! How fun it is to dream big! Or, sometimes I think how delightful it will be to be interviewed by Oprah. Big dreams? Absolutely! Will they come true? I sure hope so, but if not, I'm still 10 times further than I'd be had I never attempted to reach my big goals. Even if you don't achieve your dreams, you can still gain a lot from at least trying for them.

Stop worrying about if your endeavors, dreams, or actions will be successful and just do it. Part of living life fully is trial and error. It's only when you stop incessantly worrying about whether you'll be successful or not that you can finally achieve your goals. Don't put limits to what you're capable of doing. Even if you try something and it doesn't work, you're never a failure as long as you learned the greater lesson.

"What you get by achieving your goals is not as important as what you become by achieving your goals." Zig Ziglar

There are so many people with big dreams, yet they let fear hold them back. Year after year, they go through the motions of life, yearning to try something new, but instead letting the pain of regret build up inside of them. And before you know it one year turns into five years and five years turn into ten, and it becomes harder and harder to turn those dreams into reality. What if you never make a real effort to do something you've been dreaming to do? Don't get to be 80-years old and look back on your life thinking, *"What would have happened to my life if I would have done that?"* Most people fail because they never go for it. I don't want you to have regrets.

Never let your dreams get stolen by your fears. Each of us has our own unique dreams. Dare to go for them! Pursue them. Do not be afraid to burn your tongue in pursuit of a dream. If fear is holding you back from pursuing your dream, try imagining the regret you'll feel if you never even try. Fear of regret is stronger than fear of failure. Of course, it can be scary to get out there and risk things not working out. But you should be even more afraid of waking up years later, kicking yourself, and asking, *"What if?"*

Grounds for Thought: When you're 80-years old and looking back on your life, what will you regret *not* doing? Is there something you've been dreaming of doing that you wonder if you'd ever be able to accomplish? What would be the worst that could happen if you pushed past those fears and pursued that dream or goal? Have you ever looked at others who have embraced their dreams and goals and wished you were doing the same? Have you ever started pursuing a dream and then gave up? Why?

Grounds for Action: Set a "burn your tongue" dream for your life—a dream that seems so big or out of reach. Perhaps in your professional life, relationships, finances, health, or personal life: a vacation you want to work toward, a dream business you want to create, a desirable weight you'd like to get to, a book you'd like to write, an event you'd like to compete in, a hobby you want to master, a large debt you want to pay off, that house you'd like to buy, etc. Think of it this way: what one thing will you regret if you don't at least try to do before you die? Have the faith to believe that nothing is impossible with hard work and a strong dose of faith and courage.

"Shoot for the moon; if you miss, you'll land amongst the stars." Les Brown

The Last Cup

Never stop drinking in new life experiences. Don't get stuck like most of us do when we get older. Instead, keep that zest for trying new things. If you want to fully savor all that life can be, you're going to need to risk burning your tongue. Yes, that may mean having more failures instead of playing it safe and comfortable, but if you never take that risk, you'll never fully embrace life. We need variety, a change of pace, and new experiences to keep our brew from getting stagnant. Something out of the ordinary will give us just the jolt to wake-up our lives. You will get bored if you don't warm up your life a bit and do some out-of-the-box things to keep life exciting. Happy women take chances. They take chances when others won't.

Most of us are hesitant to try anything new for fear that we'll get it wrong. Here's what I can tell you for sure: you won't do everything right. You'll win some and you'll lose some, but that's what keeps life full of flavor. Don't let the fear of failure hold you back. Creating a life you love requires courage, commitment, and faith.

Wonderful changes take place in ourselves when we decide to spread our wings and try different things. Put yourself out there, risk making mistakes, and let them lead you one step closer to where you want to be.

Don't be one of those women who shrinks from challenges. Most people sabotage themselves by not allowing themselves to enjoy life by being so insecure they never dare to take a risk.

We all have times when things don't turn out the way we hope they will even though we did our best. That certainly doesn't make us a failure in life. We must experience setbacks to be truly successful. Failure is often necessary for real learning and growth to occur. It teaches us lessons we need to learn. It's impossible to see all that's possible in life without making a few mistakes along the way. Don't get so caught up in fearing any type of failure that you live life with little luster because you always choose to play it safe. Get out there and burn your tongue! Learn from these experiences so you can make better decisions next time around.

There are no guarantees in life. You can try to protect yourself from ever failing or feeling uncomfortable, but then you are limiting the joy in your life. Truthfully, life is enjoyed most when we challenge ourselves to take some chances. So you might as well live life to the fullest and burn your tongue along the way!

GROUND RULE #6

Choose to See Your Cup Half Full ~ Stay Positive

"Your living is determined not so much by what life brings to you as by the attitude you bring to life; not so much by what happens to you as by the way your mind looks at what happens." John Homer Miller

You Don't Need a Full Cup to Be Happy; You Just Need the Right Perspective

"What we see depends mainly on what we look for." Sir John Lubbock

Throughout our lives, our cups are constantly being emptied and filled. When our cups are being filled with good things, happy events, and positive outcomes, it's easy to be positive. When our cups are being emptied by challenges, disappointments, and negative events, it's normal to feel down. The problem comes when we spend too much time focusing on that empty cup. So many people go around negative and discouraged, allowing their circumstances to get them down. They feel they have too many problems to enjoy life so they get in the habit of making themselves miserable. Are you one of them?

If you are waiting for your problems to go away so you can finally be happy again, you're going to be waiting a long time because the truth is—there will always be something you are dealing with. When one challenge is over, another will usually arise to drain your cup again. The key to happy living is to stop waiting for your cup to be completely full—for all your problems to be gone. You can be happy and positive regardless of what life hands you. Our circumstances are just a small part of what makes us joyful. Let me give you a story to illustrate.

 **Second Cup Story:**

Two men were patients in the same hospital room. Every day the man closest to the window would share with his friend what he saw outside, describing the scene in great detail so his roommate could enjoy the view even though he was confined to his bed.

"Today I see a beautiful sunrise," he'd say. *"The kids are out there playing, the trees are blooming…"* and on and on and on. Each day the bedridden patient looked forward to hearing his friend's report on what was going on out in the world. In fact, it was the highlight of his day. One day, the patient by the window got so excited and said, *"Oh, you should see the parade coming by with a marching band and adults and kids celebrating and having such a good time!"*

After several weeks, the patient by the window passed away, and the other patient asked if he could have the bed by the window so he could see all the activity outside. The nurse agreed and she moved his bed next to the window; but when the man looked out the window, much to his surprise, all he could see was a brick wall. About 15 feet away was another wing of the hospital.

The patient called the nurse back in and said, *"Hey, wait a minute. What's going on? My friend explained all those beautiful scenes outside and I can't see anything but a wall."* The nurse smiled and said, *"Sir, didn't you realize your friend was blind? He chose to see a beautiful life from the inside out."*

See, that's the wonderful secret about life: you don't need a full cup to be happy! You just have to have the right perspective. Choosing to see your cup half full means spending less time complaining about your life and more time enjoying it. Instead of focusing and dwelling on what's not right and what you wish you could change, you focus on what's going right and how you can make the most out of what you've been given. It's about seeing the opportunities and not the obstacles in your life. Seeing your cup half full means learning to stay positive regardless of what situation you are in.

Your attitude has such a huge impact on how much you fully enjoy life. Believe me, you don't have to have a perfect life to be happy. All of us possess at least one (if not multiple) circumstances that threaten to get in the way of our happiness. You have a choice to make regarding them; let them ruin your happiness or choose to be happy in spite of them. Happy women don't have fewer problems than unhappy women; they just have a different mindset in dealing with them. Life events and experiences come and go, regardless of your preference. So you might as well choose to enjoy your days. We have to take the good with the bad. Everything may not be perfect in your life, but you've got to learn to do the best you can, with what you have, with where you are.

"I used to say, 'I sure hope things will change.' Then I learned that the only way things are going to change for me is when I change." Jim Rohn

Complaining and negativity spoil the enjoyment of your life. A bad attitude can quickly spread to all other areas. It can negatively impact your health and sabotage your level of happiness. There is proof to show that optimists are healthier and tend to live longer lives. Research shows positive thinking lowers blood pressure and stress levels and strengthens the immune system. Optimists are also more productive, have more energy, and are less depressed. Negative emotions actually take more years off your life than smoking. So the way I see it, pessimists may be right, but optimists live longer!

The fact is that happy women think differently. A shift in your perspective can take your life in an entirely new direction and create a better future for you. Refuse to let negative thinking hold you back. You have the potential to create your own fulfillment and joy. It just might mean a major attitude shift. Don't miss out on all the opportunities in your life because your focus is off. Your life will follow your thoughts. If you dwell on positive thoughts, your life will move in that direction. If you continually think negatively, you'll have a negative life. The saying is true—you have to change your thinking before you can ever change your living.

The life you have right now is the only one you have so you might as well learn to enjoy it. The day you realize you don't need a full cup to be happy is the day that will change your life. Make the most out of whatever you've been given. Start having a good attitude right where you are. When you feel good about your life, it is easier to feel good about other things. The ironic thing is, when you start to change your focus and see the half full side of your life instead of the half empty side, not only will you start to enjoy life more, but your cup actually feels fuller. Let me give you some strategies for learning to be a more positive person.

Grounds for Thought: Have you gotten into the habit of making yourself miserable? Are you waiting for your problems to go away to start being happy? Do you spend so much time complaining about your life that you've forgotten how to enjoy it?

JAVA JOLT #1
You Can Drink In Life With a Caffeinated or Decaf Attitude—The Choice is Yours

"There is little difference in people but that little difference makes a big difference. The little difference is attitude. The big difference is whether it is positive or negative." W. Clement Stone

Do you know someone with a negative attitude? I'm an optimist—I don't think there are a lot of negative people in the world, but they sure must move around a lot because I've met many of them! Perhaps you work with some of them or maybe you live with one of them? Could you possibly be one of them? The one difference in people that has the biggest effect on how much they enjoy life is their attitude. We all have both a caffeinated and decaffeinated self inside of us. Whichever attitude a person chooses to drink in life with makes a huge difference in their happiness and enjoyment level. The reality is whichever attitude we choose to fill most often is what we will be.

It's amazing how people can approach life from such different perspectives. Decaf people are the cup half empty types. They are the ones who constantly complain about their lives, criticize or discourage others, always focus on what's going wrong, and what they don't have. Decaf people tend to see what's missing in life rather than what's going right. Caffeinated people, on the other hand, are uplifting and energizing. They focus on their possibilities and what is going right, speak well of others, and generally can find happiness in any situation, regardless of their circumstances. The first step to being a more positive person is to identify which type of attitude you're currently drinking in life— caffeinated or decaffeinated? Your attitude could be keeping you from living your best life and you may not even realize it.

Many people mistakenly believe that their attitude is set. That it's part of the hand they've been dealt at birth. That some of us are born positive and some of us are born negative. That simply is not true! Oh sure, some people may naturally be more positive, smile more, and laugh more, but anyone can train themselves to be a caffeinated person. Your attitude is a truly a *choice*. You see in life what you want to see. If you haven't noticed, however, thinking positively doesn't come naturally. It's much more natural to speak negatively about our lives—to focus on the things that we don't have, that aren't going well, and that bother us. We have to purposely choose to shift our focus from half empty to half full because it simply does not happen on its own. I believe it takes the same amount of effort to make yourself happy or miserable. So why not choose to make yourself happy? Learn a lesson from this story.

 Second Cup Story:

A 92-year old, petite, well-poised lady was fully dressed by 8 a.m. this morning, with her hair fashionably styled and her make-up perfectly applied. Today was a big day in her life, the day she was moving to a nursing home for her husband of nearly 70 years had recently passed away, making the move necessary because she was legally blind.

After many hours of waiting patiently in the lobby of the nursing home, she smiled sweetly when told her room was finally ready. As she maneuvered her walker to the elevator, a nurse provided a visual description of her tiny room, including the eyelet sheets that had been hung on her window. *"I love it,"* she stated emphatically. The nurse replied *"But Mrs. Jones, you haven't even seen it yet. Wait until you see the furniture."*

The elderly lady responded, *"That doesn't have anything to do with it,"* she replied. *"Happiness is something you decide on ahead of time. Whether I like my room or not doesn't depend on how the furniture is arranged...it's how I choose to arrange my mind."*

You alone are responsible for your attitude—not other people or negative circumstances. For many of us, this is a disappointing thought because it's easier to blame someone or something else for our bad attitude—our job, our parents, our spouse, the weather, our health, a tragedy. It's true that all these can threaten to push down our attitude, but they only have the power that we give them. Abraham Lincoln was wise when he said, *"Most folks are about as happy as they make up their minds to be."*

If you have lost joy in your journey of life, perhaps it is because you have allowed a bad attitude to seep into you. Have you gotten in the habit of making yourself unhappy—looking at others around you, all you can see is what they have—a better car, a bigger home, a more exciting job, well-behaved kids, a better looking husband, fewer struggles? Listen to yourself. Have you stopped seeing your cup half full and instead started complaining about the things you don't have, you're lacking, that aren't going right, or you're dissatisfied with? Sure, it's easy to go around comparing your life to those who seem to have so much more than you, but there are so many people who have so much less than you and would love to have what you do.

We have so much going right in our lives, too. Often our focus is so off that we completely miss the good things. You may not have the perfect job, but thank God that you are employed. Some would love to have your job. Your house may seem too small, and it may not be your dream home, but thank God you have a roof over your head. You may not be married to the perfect spouse, but thank God you have someone you love. Do you know how many people are lonely today? (Believe it or not, some woman would be glad to have your husband!) Yes, your house might be a mess, but doesn't that mean you have enough possessions to make it cluttered? And the dishes might be piled up in the sink, but doesn't that mean we had enough food to eat? If you go around complaining about these kinds of things then it's time you start drinking in life with a fresh attitude.

When we complain about our lives, we fail to see all the wonderful things that are still in front of us. The positive, good aspects of our lives sit unobserved and unappreciated. The fact is, you need to learn to see past the negative stuff if you are going to enjoy all life has to offer. Let me illustrate.

 Second Cup Story:

There's a man who lived in a beautiful house on a large lot filled with huge oak trees. In the fall when the leaves would change colors, he'd have the most breathtaking view from his large picture windows.

One day he invited a couple of friends over to enjoy the spectacular view of the red, orange, and yellow foliage. He pointed out the window to the trees in the distance and said, *"Look! Isn't it gorgeous?"* He waited for a few seconds and when he didn't get any response, he turned to them to see if something was the matter. He noticed one of them was frowning.

"What's wrong?" he asked.

One friend responded, *"Can't you see all those fingerprints on the glass?"*

Many of us are like that friend, too focused on the problems of life to see the beauty right in front of us. But if you get too stuck on those fingerprints, you'll never experience true fulfillment. The great news is that it's never too late to change your attitude. If you've been negative and pessimistic, you can still change. If you've spent years focusing on what's wrong, it's hard to get past that. But the good news is, you *can* reprogram your mind. You can get rid of your negative mentality and develop and attitude of happiness. You have a choice to be negative or positive, but you've got to do your part to bring out the caffeinated attitude.

"The pessimist sees the difficulty in every opportunity; the optimist sees the opportunity in every difficulty." Winston Churchill

We each get to choose our outlook on life. Some will look for what's negative; others will look for what's positive. Which will you choose? There are enough pessimists and realists in the world. We don't need more negativity and decaf thinkers. The world needs more optimists, encouragers, and inspirers. Here's the plain truth: no one likes hanging around a decaf person. Your friends, family, and co-workers don't want to hear about your problems all of the time. They have enough issues to deal with of their own. If you're always talking about what's wrong or how bad your circumstances are, that's a selfish way to live. Quit living with this decaffeinated attitude. A positive attitude will improve your personal relationships more than you will ever realize.

Today I want to encourage you to be a caffeinated person. People love being around those who make them feel good about themselves and their lives. Always focus more on what's going *right* than what's going *wrong*. Being a caffeinated or decaffeinated person is not chance, but choice. You are the only person who can decide if your cup is half full or half empty. You can decide right now to have a positive or negative outlook on life. Which will you choose? Remember, your happiness rests on your decision. Today's a fresh cup. Is yours half full or half empty?

Grounds for Thought: Do you know anyone with a negative attitude? Are you a complainer? Do you focus too much on the negative side of things? Do you build others up or tear them down? Think back to the past few conversations you've had with your closest friends and family. Did the conversation turn into a pity party about what you don't have and what's bothering you about your life?

Grounds for Action: Try to go one whole day without complaining and see how you do. For the next 24 hours, deliberately speak optimistic about everything: your job, your health, your kids, and your future. This may be difficult because our natural tendency is to speak pessimistically. What helps me is to wear a rubber band on my wrist so when I catch myself complaining, I snap it. What will your wrist look like at the end of the day? Give it a try! Once you've gone a day without complaining, then try to go a week! Make a commitment to fully own your attitude. Declare to yourself that you will be a caffeinated person.

JAVA JOLT #2:
It's Not About the Brew; It's About the View

"Do not let what you cannot do interfere with what you can do." John Wooden

You might find yourself thinking, *"I know I should have a better attitude, but I've been through a lot in life. It's just not fair."* I realize things have not gone perfectly for you, but that isn't an excuse for you to wallow in self-pity and negativity. Those excuses will cause you to remain stuck right where you are and to remain a victim of your circumstances. Every single one of us has circumstances we'd like to change in our life or events we wish we didn't have to go through. If our attitude was dependent upon our circumstances, nobody would be a positive person. Yet, lots of people face situations similar to yours and have done so with a positive attitude. This confirms that in life, it's not what happens to us that will determine our happiness; it's how we react to what happens. It is up to *you* to change more than it is to change your circumstances. After all, it's really not about the brew; it's about the view. You can't control what happens to you, so it's up to you to do the best with the life you've been given.

"You can't control the direction of the wind, but you can control the sails." Dolly Parton

Life is filled with unexpected challenges, heartbreaks, failures, and disappointments. It's how we take them and what we do with them that really matters in the end. Learn to accept the hand you've been dealt, including those things you cannot change and make the most of the rest of your life. Acceptance is so important. We have to adjust to the events that are beyond our control. We can't control what happens *to* us in life, but we have complete control over what happens *in* us. It is our job to make something good from what we've been given, regardless of our circumstances. We can learn a lot from this inspiring true example.

 Second Cup Story:

Patrick Henry Hughes has been wheelchair-bound and blind since birth. By his first birthday, his mother noticed a unique gift for playing piano. By the age of two, Patrick was able to play songs like, *You Are My Sunshine* and *Twinkle, Twinkle Little Star.*

Well today, Patrick attends the University of Louisville, excelling in his studies while also playing trumpet in the marching band. How is that possible, you ask? Patrick's dad (who he calls his hero) works the graveyard shift at UPS so he can attend college with Patrick during the day. After class, he is out on the football field pushing Patrick's wheelchair so he can be in the marching band.

The most unbelievable part is Patrick's attitude. This is what he has to say about life, *"God made me blind and unable to walk. Big deal! He also gave me the ability...the musical gifts I have...the great opportunity to meet new people."*

Patrick chooses to focus on the brew he's been given; not the one he wishes he had. He's not letting what he cannot do interfere with what he can do. You see, it's our view (perspective), not our brew (our circumstances) that determines our happiness in life. Things turn out best for those who make the best of their situations. Have you been focusing too much on what you don't have, what you can't do, what you've lost, and what's wrong with your life? You need to take your eyes off your circumstances. You don't see the possibilities for your life when your eyes are only focused on your circumstances. You may need to brew up a fresh perspective. Look for hidden blessings even in difficult situations. Learn to use your situation to make you better, not bitter.

"Regardless of your lot in life, you can build something beautiful on it." Zig Ziglar

Instead of dwelling on the negative, uncontrollable aspects of your life, learn to grab hold of the things you *do* have control over—your attitude and perspective in any situation. Choose to see the possibilities; not the problems. Embrace what you've been given, what you still have, and what is going right instead of what you've lost, what's missing and what's going wrong. Seeing your cup half full means making the best of your situation—you may not like it, you may not understand it, and it may not seem fair, but you don't have to dwell on that. Keep your attitude positively focused. Even in your most miserable days, hold the attitude that tomorrow will probably be better.

There will be times when we may not like how our lives have gone, but that doesn't mean we still can't be in love with life. One of my favorite quotes states: *"Life is not about waiting for the storms to pass…it's about learning to dance in the rain."* We all face adversity; it's not the adversity, but how we react to it that will determine the happiness in our life. In your toughest times, do you spend too much time feeling sorry for yourself, or can you, by adjusting your attitude, learn to dance in the rain?

Maintaining optimism while navigating the ups and downs of life involves choosing a certain mindset. We need to accept the circumstances of our lives, and adjust to the events that are beyond our control, regardless if they seem fair to us or not. Don't get stuck on asking yourself, *"Why me?"* It's not just *you* because everyone faces difficulties sooner or later. Most likely you'll never get an answer to that question anyway, and even if you did, would it change anything? No, it wouldn't. Your circumstances would still be the same. Instead of asking,

"Why me?" it's time to ask *"How?"* *"How can I take the hand I've been dealt and make the most out of it?"*

"Don't wish it was easier; wish you were better. Don't wish for less problems; wish for more skills. Don't wish for less challenges; wish for more wisdom." Jim Rohn

Having a positive attitude doesn't mean that you will be immune to pain, frustration, or disappointment. There are still going to be days, even months, when life will be darn right painful and unpleasant. We all have hard things we're dealing with, but those who view life with a positive attitude tend to bounce back more quickly from adversity than others. If you lose a job, you can choose to see this as a defeat or as an opportunity. Who knows what else is out there until you take the time to look? And, many of us don't do that unless life pushes us. You can feel sorry for yourself, or you can choose to be challenged. When you lose a precious loved one, you can feel hopeless and powerless and just live in your grief feeling cursed for your loss. Or you can also choose to see how blessed you were to have wonderful and strong memories with this person. You can live in the sadness of your loss, or you can live with an attitude of hope knowing that death isn't the end; it's the beginning of life evermore and that your precious loved one is at peace in a more wonderful place. Do you see how your attitude can completely change your experience? If you're thinking defeating thoughts, change your thoughts to new and positive ones. This is critical in overcoming difficulties and learning to live fully once again.

"The way I see it, if you want the rainbow, you gotta put up with the rain." Dolly Parton

Like it or not, you can't control your circumstances nor can you change them. So quit allowing them to drain the joy out of living. Make every effort to deal with them and move forward. Life is too short to live it negatively. You can choose to be happy in spite of your adversities. Remember, it's not about the brew; it's about the view. Your cup can still be half full regardless of what happens in your life. There's a famous saying by Chuck Swindoll that says, *"Life is 10% what happens to you and 90% how you react to it."* How will you choose to respond to your life and the challenges before you? The choice is yours. Always choose to see your cup half full!

"I am responsible. Although I may not be able to prevent the worst from happening, I am responsible for my attitude toward the inevitable misfortunes that darken life. Bad things do happen; how I respond to them defines my character and the quality of my life. I can choose to sit in perpetual sadness, immobilized by the gravity of my loss, or I can choose to rise from the pain and treasure the most precious gift I have - life itself."
Walter Anderson

Grounds for Thought: Do you keep a positive outlook during difficult times? Are you allowing your circumstances to dull your enthusiasm for life and keep you in a negative frame of mind? Is there a situation in your life right now that you can look at from a fresh perspective? Where have you been placing your focus—on your problems or your possibilities? Are you waiting for something to change in your life before you can finally start enjoying it?

Grounds for Action: It's time to brew up a fresh perspective. No matter how down and out you feel at times, there are certain things that *are* working in your life. So instead of dwelling on the negative, take a moment to consider what is working. Grab a sheet of paper and draw a line down the middle. In the first column, spend some time writing out all the positive aspects of your life. Think of those things going well in each of the key Life Cup areas: relationships, career/life work, physical health, finances, helping others, spiritual, fun, and personal growth. Then do the same with negative things on the second column. Which column gets most of your attention? Whenever you get down, re-read the list of positives. It will help you shift your focus from a more negative one to a more positive one. Focus on the possibility side not the problem side. You'll soon see that your cup is half full. The more you focus on seeing the good in your life, the more motivated and inspired you feel about life.

JAVA JOLT #3:
Limit Your Time with Decaf People—They Can Easily Empty Your Cup

"Some cause happiness wherever they go; others <u>whenever</u> they go." Oscar Wilde

Did you know that you are just as likely to catch someone's bad attitude as you are their cold? That's right, attitudes are contagious! One pessimist can bring down 10 optimists faster than 10 optimists can bring one pessimist up! Negative people are energy drainers. And they impact us more than we probably realize. To develop a more positive attitude, you must not only start by looking in the mirror, but you also need to look at the people around you. The people you spend the most time with greatly impact your outlook on life. We become like those people we most hang around with. If those closest to you are positive (caffeinated) people, they help to keep your cup full. If those around you are negative (decaf) people they will drag you down.

Every time you interact with someone, they are either filling or emptying you. It is very difficult to keep a good attitude when those around you are always draining your emotional reserves. I'm sure you know your share of decaf people continually threatening to drain the life right out of you. Those people who are always complaining, blaming, judging others, gossiping, and talking about how bad things are. If there are people in your life who simply by calling you, bring tension and stress to your day, then minimize your time with them. Limit your time with decaf people because they can easily empty your cup.

Astonishingly, there are people in this world who seem to thrive on being unhappy! I'm sure you've met one (or many)—that person who loves to let you know about their ever-building list of problems. (You have enough problems of your own—you don't need someone else to drag you down!) Some people will just simply choose to live negatively. As much as you'd like to, there's nothing you or anyone else can do to change their attitude for them. They've gotten into the habit of making themselves miserable and they prefer to stay there. Fine. But you don't need to let them bring you down. You can still choose to be a positive, caffeinated person. Too many of us are drawn down because someone in our life is negative. Don't allow someone else to rob you of happiness.

Instead, start interacting with more caffeinated people—those who have a positive outlook on life. Those whose joy rubs off on you, leaving you happier, more encouraged and more positive than you were before. People who are positive, uplifting, and nourishing are the ones who help fill your cup. They radiate a warmth and positive energy that makes us love to be around them because they raise our spirits. These are friends and family members who see their cup half full, but who also carry a pot to fill others' while they are at it. Make a conscious effort to surround yourself with caffeinated people. Whether that's at work, volunteer opportunities, your own Inspirational Coffee Club, meeting a positive friend for coffee, or calling someone who always makes you feel good. As you associate with these kinds of people, their positivity tends to rub off on you. Attitudes are contagious. Get infected with a positive one!

The truth is, you may not be able to get away from all the decaf people around you, especially if they live with you and work with you. But, the more negative those closest to you are, even more important it is for you to bring more caffeinated, positive types into your life everyday! Surround yourself with others who balance out their negativity. Do whatever you can so that you aren't allowing decaf people around you to empty your cup. Don't let someone else choose your attitude for you.

Grounds for Thought: Does your environment fill you or empty you? Do you mainly hang around complainers? Is there anyone around you that you're allowing to get you down? Do you need to start surrounding yourself with more positive people?

Grounds for Action: Make a list of all the people you spend time with on a regular basis (family, friends, and co-workers). Put a 'C' next to the Caffeinated ones (those who uplift you, encourage you, and see the positive). Put a 'D' next to the Decaffeinated ones (those who discourage, criticize, and see the negative). Do you see a pattern? Are you constantly surrounded by nay-sayers? Determine who is the most positive person(s) on your list and spend more time with them. You most likely cannot completely abandon yourself from negative people around you, but you can get closer to the positive ones so that when you go back to the negative ones, you do not as easily submit to their negativity.

JAVA JOLT #4:
Refill Your Attitude Regularly

"You must start with a positive attitude or you will surely end without one." Carrie Latet

There is no way to overstate the importance of a positive attitude in your life. However, no one can underestimate the difficulty in maintaining it. You can make a decision to have a positive attitude, but if you don't make plans to manage your attitude every day, then you are likely to end up back where you started. It's like the wise farmer says, *"The hardest thing about cows is they never stay milked."* Our attitude is just like that. It will not stay set. Keeping a positive attitude takes continual refilling because, quite frankly, life can take a toll on us. It's so easy to become emptied throughout our days. Here's a perfect illustration.

**Second Cup Story:**

Our attitude is similar to a helium-filled balloon. For the first few days, the balloon looks cheerful and full of life. Over the course of a couple of days, however, the balloon begins to shrink, gradually sinking lower and lower until it finally lands on the floor, completely deflated. If only we refilled that balloon with a daily dose of helium, that balloon would continue to look beautiful and last for months.

The same is true for our attitude. We may make a great effort to begin our days positively, but throughout the day, it's easy to get emptied. You get a flat tire on the way to work. Your attitude is emptied. You get to work only to realize you missed an important meeting. It is emptied a bit more. You get to daycare and are told your son misbehaved all day. Now you're even more emptied. You get home at the end of the day, and you notice the cat got sick all over the living room carpet. It's official—you're emptied! We need to continue refilling ourselves throughout the day so we can keep our cups half full, especially on those tough days. If you don't continually fill yourself up, the pressures of life will empty you completely. You've got to make sure you've got more positive than negative throughout the day. So how do you do that?

Start by getting up each morning and setting your mind in the right direction. Decide that you are going to enjoy each day. Put a smile on your face and expect good things. No matter what comes your way, you can still keep a positive outlook. Every day, choose to live with an attitude that expects good things to happen to you. We can all learn a lesson from the following story.

 **Second Cup Story:**

There once was a woman who woke up one morning, looked in the mirror, and noticed she had only three hairs left on her head. *"Well,"* she said, *"I think I'll braid my hair today."* So she did and she had a wonderful day.

The next day she woke up, looked in the mirror and saw that she had only two hairs left on her head. *"H-M-M,"* she said, *"I think I'll part my hair down the middle today."* So she did and she had a grand day.

The next day she woke up, looked in the mirror and noticed that she had only one hair left on her head. *"Well,"* she said, *"Today I'm going to wear my hair in a pony tail."* So she did and she had a fun, fun day.

The next day she woke up, looked in the mirror and noticed that there wasn't a single hair on her head. *"YEAH!"* she exclaimed, *"I don't have to fix my hair today!"*

We get to decide every day the attitude we will embrace for that day: we can rise and shine or we can rise and whine, and shining is the best way to go through life. Yet how many of us really wake up naturally upbeat and positive, feeling this is going to be a great day for us? It's much more natural for us to wake up and say, *"I don't want to go to work today!"* or *"I don't want to get out of bed!"*

You have a choice: you can spend the morning in bed recounting the things about your job you dread or get out of bed and be thankful you have a job as so many would love the opportunity to have yours. You can spend the morning criticizing the saddlebags on your thighs and how your pants just seem to be getting tighter and tighter, or be thankful for legs that work. A paraplegic would gladly take your legs, saddlebags and all. Each day is a gift, and as long as your eyes open for another day, you should focus on the opportunities of the new day.

Here's my first recommendation for you: each day when you get up (before you lift your head off the pillow), put a smile on your face and say, *"I'm going to have a great day!"* instead of the usual, *"I don't want to go to work* or *I don't want to get out of bed."* Set your day in the right direction. If you think that sounds silly, here's another way to look at it. So often we say things like, *"I have to go to work today," "I have to take the kids to practice." "I have to make breakfast." "I have to take the car in for an oil change." "I have to see my family this weekend."* We act as if we're burdened by so much of the activity in our lives. But the reality is that if we are gifted another day, we *get* to do those things. We get to live this life while so many have left this world far too early. We get to drive in traffic while so many are too sick to drive a car. We get to go to a job while so many are unemployed. We get to raise our children even if they drive us crazy at times. We get to interact with our employees and customers and make a difference in their lives. We get to care for our aging parents while so many wish they could have more time with theirs. We get to eat three meals a day while millions of people are starving. Be completely honest with yourself: are you a 'get to' or a 'have to' person?

My second challenge for you is to learn to apply the "Cup Half Full Habit" to your life throughout the day. It's a great technique that I use to help me change my thinking. If we don't watch ourselves, our daily conversations will too easily turn into complaining about stress in work and life. We need to train ourselves to focus more on the bright side. During the times you find yourself complaining about something—a messy house, a bad day, an achy back, a difficult project, a harsh customer—as soon as you've poured out your frustrations, then say, *"Ok, enough complaining. It's time to see my cup half full."* And follow your complaining with something positive.

The "Cup Half Full Habit" helps you focus on what's *right* in your life instead of focusing only on what's *wrong*. No matter what your troubles, there are still plenty of things going right. We can complain about the road construction, but aren't we grateful for the street crews who keep our travel smooth? We can complain about the dishwasher needing to be unloaded, but aren't we grateful we didn't have to wash them by hand? We can complain about running our children to and from sports practice and events, but aren't we glad our children are healthy enough to participate in these things? We can complain about having to wash clothes, but shouldn't we be glad we've got more than one outfit to wear?

We can complain about the leaves that need raking and the lawn that needs mowing, but doesn't that mean we have a home?

I recently found myself complaining about locking my keys in my car on my dad's birthday. Frustrated, mad, and impatient, I calmed myself by applying the "Cup Half Full Habit"...I am so glad I have AAA auto club membership, I am so glad I have my cell phone, I am so glad I had an extra hour and a half with my dad. And once the tow truck came and the keys were back in my hands, I had a renewed appreciation for my car and the mobility it allows me.

Applying the "Cup Half Full Habit" to your life will change your attitude in a hurry throughout the day. We all slip into a pity party once in awhile. After all, we're only human. The important thing is to cut the pity party short so we don't get stuck in that attitude of negativity. Think of your life like a cup of coffee. Each negative word empties your cup more and more until you reach a point where you can no longer see it half full anymore. Living with an optimistic attitude throughout the day will give you a fresh perspective on the good things around you. I assure you—for every negative thing, you can find a positive. A "Cup Half Full Habit" will bring you far more happiness and contentment in life. Try it and see!

Grounds for Thought: Do you get up each morning excited about your day? Are you a 'have to' or 'get to' person? Were you able to go a day without complaining?

Grounds for Action: When you get up each morning, smile and enthusiastically say out loud, *"Today's going to be a great day!"* It may seem awkward at first, but you'll have a noticeable difference in your attitude. Then, throughout the day, apply the "Cup Half Full Habit" to your life. Whenever a negative statement or thought is expressed, counter it with a positive one. It takes about 30 days to make a habit stick, so try the "Cup Half Full Habit" for a month and see the positive affect it has on your outlook.

The Last Cup

What we think and focus on sets the course of our life. You can alter your life simply by altering your attitude. How will you choose to see your life from this moment? Half full or half empty? The choice is yours and yours alone. Being able to choose our attitude is truly one of the greatest of our life's privileges. If you want to get serious about being happy, you need to choose a joyful attitude.

Everything may not be perfect in your life, but if you don't learn to be happy where you are, you will never get to where you want to be. Life isn't always fair, but it can still be pretty darn good! One of the best-known strategies for a more successful, happier life is to pour out negative thoughts and refill yourself with new, positive ones. This change in perspective can change your whole life. The way you see the world has a heavy impact on your happiness level. Don't miss out on all the opportunities in your life because your focus is off. Your life will follow your thoughts. The more you focus on what's missing, the more you start to feel unsatisfied and unhappy. Once you start focusing on the glass being half empty, that's all you start to see.

There will always be difficulties in life. There will always be negative people. How you choose to let them affect you is completely up to you. Inspire others with a positive attitude. You will notice a marked difference in your happiness level. I *choose* to see my cup half full. Will you? If you're still having trouble, maybe this poem will help you.

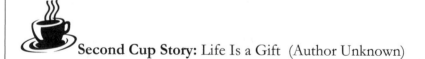**Second Cup Story:** Life Is a Gift (Author Unknown)

Today before you think of saying an unkind word -
  Think of someone who can't speak.
Before you complain about the taste of your food -
  Think of someone who has nothing to eat.
Before you complain about your husband or wife -
  Think of someone who's crying out to God for a companion.
Today before you complain about life -
  Think of someone who went too early to heaven.
Before you complain about your children -

Think of someone who desires children but they're barren.
Before you argue about your dirty house, someone didn't clean or sweep -
  Think of the people who are living in the streets.
Before whining about the distance you drive -
  Think of someone who walks the same distance with their feet.
And when you are tired and complain about your job -
  Think of the unemployed, the disabled who wished they had your job.
And when depressing thoughts seem to get you down -
  Put a smile on your face and thank God you're alive and still around.

"When you change the way you look at things, the things you look at eventually begin to change." Wayne Dyer

GROUND RULE #7

You're Never Guaranteed Another Cup ~ Savor Each Day

"For yesterday is but a memory and tomorrow is only a vision; but today well lived makes every yesterday a memory of happiness and every tomorrow a vision of hope."
Sanskrit Poem

Drink in Life by Cherishing Each Day!

"Yesterday is history. Tomorrow a mystery. Today is a gift. That's why they call it the present." Unknown

I am noticing that the older I get, the more the days slip by all too quickly. I'm sure you can relate. As adults we become so busy and distracted trying to keep up with everyday life that it's easy to lose sight of the preciousness of each day. When we are rushing through life, sometimes we forget that our life is going to end one day. None of us knows how soon that one day will be, but we know our time on earth is ticking. The important question is: *How are you going to live until then?* We need to remember that each day truly is a gift since we are never assured tomorrow will come. The truth is this—not a single one of us is guaranteed another cup. To live our fullest lives, we need to drink in life by cherishing each and every day we're given. Life is not about living longer—it's about living better. We can learn a great lesson from this man's inspiring true story.

**Second Cup Story:**

I recently saw a speech on the Internet given by a college professor named Randy Paush who was diagnosed with inoperable pancreatic cancer. I've learned that Randy has passed away since this speech, and his final lecture to his students has been turned into a best-selling book called *'The Last Lecture.'* In this particular speech, the professor was speaking nine months after his diagnosis in which he had only been given three months to live. Upon witnessing his extra months of life someone said to him, *"Wow, you're really beating the grim reaper."*

His reply is one I will never forget: *"You don't beat the reaper by living longer; you beat the reaper by living well and living fully. For the reaper will come for all of us. The question is what do we do by the time we are born and the time he shows up? When he shows up, it's too late for us."*

Are you waiting for some kind of a wake-up call before you start to enjoy your life? If so, consider this to be it. Unlike the freshness date on a canister of coffee, you aren't born with an expiration date stamped on you. If we somehow knew when we were destined to leave this earth, it would make most of us appreciate more fully the days we live on it. Our life is such a gift, but many of us wait to live our days more fully until we're faced with our own mortality. Then we wonder why we waited so long to start enjoying ourselves, and we yearn for that time back so we can start living differently. But you can never get time back. Don't wait for a crisis or illness before you start to enjoy each day of your life. Get out there and get to living *now*! You can't control the length of your life, but you can control its depth and quality.

Ironically, time is our most precious resource, but it's also the one we waste most. Instead, we take most days for granted and don't even think twice about throwing our time away. Have you ever found yourself saying, *"I'm just trying to waste some time?"* We can never get back the time that's gone. Once a day's gone, it's gone. Stop wasting your precious days! Each day we have is a gift. Once it's over it can never be recaptured no matter how badly we wish it could. Remember there are no do-overs in life. Are you spending your time wisely?

"Somebody should tell us, right at the start of our lives that we are dying. Then we might live life to the limit, every minute of every day. Do it! I say. Whatever you want to do, do it now! There are only so many tomorrows." Michael Landon

Remember, you need to drink in life one day at a time—sip by sip, not gulp by gulp. It's time to start living as if each day is a gift. Decide today you will not waste another day. You never know when your last cup will come. Your clock is ticking, so take the time you have left and make it count! Following are some tips for making every day more sacred.

Grounds for Thought: No matter what your age, looking back on your life to this point, can you honestly say you've enjoyed life as fully as you could have? Are you pleased with how you've been spending your time? Do you treasure each day? Or do you allow each new day to come and go, a carbon copy of the one before, basically unnoticed, unappreciated, and under-used? If you knew exactly when your 'expiration date' was, how would that information lead you to live differently?

JAVA JOLT #1:
You Can't Enjoy the Current Cup if You Are Still Focused on the Last

"Your past has passed. Your future begins today." Unknown

There is nothing more damaging to your enjoyment of today than spending your present time dwelling on the past. Even though you may want to move forward in your life, you simply cannot move ahead and enjoy each day fully when you are still focused on the past. Whatever has happened is over. Good or bad, it has passed. Each morning is a new day and a new cup of opportunities is poured. You are not your past. It's good to use your past to instruct you and to help make you a wiser woman going forward, but don't let it keep you stuck there. Look back for lessons in the first cup, but not for regrets. You can't enjoy your current cup if you're still focusing on the last. Think of it this way.

Second Cup Story:

The car you drive has a large windshield but only a relatively small rearview mirror. The implication is obvious—what happens in your past is not nearly as important as what happens in your future. Where you are going is much more important than where you have been. If you only stay focused on your past, you're likely to miss many new opportunities ahead. Remember, you can't move forward when you're still looking backwards. Quit dwelling over something you can't change. You need to let go of the old before you can have a new beginning.

Often we look back at our past and see everything we wish we could take back—a cup overflowing with our mistakes, regrets, and 'should have's.' We need to learn to pour out our hurts, pain, regrets, and mistakes and remember that yesterday is history. You'll never forget it, but you need to move past it so you're not living in it. The energy it takes to hang onto the past holds you back from enjoying today. You need to start drinking in today fully without letting your past get in the way. You can't expect today or tomorrow to be better if you're still thinking about yesterday.

"Sometimes it's holding on that makes one strong, but sometimes it's letting go."
Sylvia Robinson

If you dwell on old mistakes and replay past failures, or if you go about wondering what might have been, you are wasting good energy that could be focused on today. If you did something that you are ashamed of, that you regret, or that you're sorry about, understand one thing: with your awareness at the time, you did the best you could. So stop feeling so guilty. You wouldn't repeat it, so start forgiving yourself. Give up hoping for a better past, a second chance, or a do-over. The past has passed. There is nothing you can do differently. So many of us want to blank out the present and look to the past. We deeply want to turn back the clock and reverse what happened. The honest-to-goodness truth is you can't do anything about your past, but you can still do so much about your future.

If you truly want to savor today, then wherever you are, in either good situations or bad, you need to learn to appreciate your life each day. Maybe something unfair has happened—financial struggles, loss of a loved one, or a failed relationship. Still, that doesn't give you the right to throw away today. Accept the situations you cannot change and embrace today. Remember, your life isn't finished yet. Despite what happened in your past, get back up and move forward. What matters now is how you live your life from this point forward.

Each morning you wake up, God is giving you a fresh start. Let today be a new beginning. Step forward into a fresh future. If you're filled with regrets, pains, and hurts from you last cup, you need to pour them out so you can start focusing on today's cup. Refuse to waste any more of your precious days focused on the past. Quit looking back. You can't fully enjoy today when you're still focusing on yesterday's cup.

"Yesterday is not ours to recover, but tomorrow is ours to win or to lose." Lyndon B. Johnson

Grounds for Thought: Why is it so difficult sometimes to let go of the past? Have you been spending too much of your precious time looking back? What circumstances cause you to look back? What do you need to let go of in order to start focusing more on today? What regrets, rejections, mistakes, and resentments do you need to overcome? How can you use these events to help you see the importance of savoring each day?

Grounds for Action: Pour out yesterday's old brew. Grab an unused coffee filter (or a sheet of paper for you non-coffee drinkers) and write down every regret, failure, and disappointment you are still dwelling on. If you could do anything over in life, what would it be? Once you've poured out your guilt and regrets onto that filter, crumple it up, throw it away, and realize you can't change the past. Make today a fresh start. Say out loud, *"I am emptying my mind of regrets because I know I can't change the past, but I won't let it destroy my present."*

JAVA JOLT #2:
Worry Bitters the Enjoyment of Your Current Cup

"I am not afraid of tomorrow, for I have seen yesterday and I love today." William Allen White

Just as people dwell over yesterday, we so easily slip into a mode of worrying constantly about tomorrow. Stop letting yourself be upset, afraid, and anxious. You may say, *"Well, I just can't help it!"* but the truth is, we can learn to control our emotions if we choose to. Constantly worrying about tomorrow not only leads to unhappiness in the short term, but we miss an opportunity to really love and appreciate our life where we are, right now, right in front of us. Worry only bitters the enjoyment of our current cup.

Worry is such a waste of precious time and energy. Worrying about things we cannot control robs us of contentment now. Seldom do the things we fear come to pass. In our minds, we are projecting things that will likely never occur. Maybe this will help you—92% of the time the things we worry about never even happen. Worrying won't change the outcome…and pretty soon all those precious moments will have slipped away. If you live your life worried about all the 'what ifs,' you'll never enjoy what is happening in the present.

"Today is the tomorrow you worried about yesterday. Was it worth it?" Unknown

 **Second Cup Story:**

Two adult friends were sitting at a table in the mall food court talking about all the things they've been going through lately. The one said to the other, *"It just seems that my life is full of problems. And just as I get through one, another surfaces."*

Suddenly, they heard a soft voice say, *"But what about all the days in between?"*

They quickly turned around and saw two teenage girls sitting behind them. *"I said it,"* one of the girls acknowledged. *"I asked about what happens to all the days in between?"*

Curious, the friends asked the young lady to explain. *"Well, this is just my opinion, but people are always thinking about their problems. What about all those days in between? Those days we throw away worrying about what happened or what might happen?"* She continued, *"Those days in between are good days, and we probably have more of those than the bad ones but we waste them!"*

Are you throwing away the days in between? Today, most interestingly, most of us would probably focus more time on how we spend 24 dollars versus how we spend 24 hours. But our time is actually a more precious asset than our money. Your time is completely non-refundable. You can never buy more, and you can't get those hours back when they're gone.

Don't throw away your time! Our days aren't in endless supply.

Before you start worrying about something, ask yourself, *"Is this worth my time?"* Most situations simply aren't worthy of using up your precious time. Too often in life we worry about issues that work themselves out over time. Worrying is a waste of time, energy, and life itself. Think about this...an hour a day spent worrying equates to more than two weeks from your life. That's two weeks that could have instead been lived, enjoyed, and celebrated. How sad!

"One day at a time--this is enough. Do not look back and grieve over the past for it is gone; and do not be troubled about the future, for it has not yet come. Live in the present, and make it so beautiful it will be worth remembering." Unknown

Worrying, just like regretting, is a habit that can be broken. Just as you need to pour out the regrets of your past so you can start fresh tomorrow, you also need to pour out your worries and anxieties along with them. But how, you ask? The best way I know to do that is to turn your worries and regrets over to God. Ask for help so you don't have to carry your anxieties alone. Practice emptying your mind daily before you go to sleep at night by taking them to God in prayer. Then, learn to trust God to take care of the future so you can be more content with today. You do not have to worry about what may happen tomorrow when you remember that God is already there.

With every new day comes new opportunities. Each day brings a fresh cup of life. Stop analyzing the past, stop worrying about your future, and choose to live in the moment. When you do this, you are able to be present for your life and not only will you feel better, but you also make space for great things to come into your life.

"Therefore do not worry about tomorrow, for tomorrow will worry about itself. Each day has enough trouble of its own." Matthew 6:34

Grounds for Thought: What circumstances are causing you to feel fearful or worried? Are you bogging your mind down with worries about tomorrow? What do you need to let go of so you can start enjoying today?

Grounds for Action: Start emptying your mind every night. Put a journal by your bedside and each evening write in it all the worries and anxieties you are feeling. Then, say a prayer and remember that you don't have to worry about tomorrow because God is already there.

JAVA JOLT #3:
Overcome Your "Second Cup Addiction"

"For a long time it had seemed to me that life was about to begin - real life. But there was always some obstacle in the way, something to be gotten through first, some unfinished business, time still to be served, a debt to be paid. Then life would begin. At last it dawned on me that these obstacles were my life." Alfred Souza

There's a natural tendency for people to put off enjoying life today because they've convinced themselves there will be a better time to enjoy themselves in the future. We tend to pin our happiness and joy on future outcomes. We tell ourselves we'll be happy when we get married, we get some debts paid off, we retire, we get a bigger house, we have children, we get a better job, we get that degree, our business is flourishing, the kids start behaving and on and on. I call this our "Second Cup Addiction." Our lives always seem to be about tomorrow. We're always waiting for the next cup to be happy. We rob ourselves of precious time today when we're always chasing happiness as an event we'll get to in the future. We promise ourselves that once this event happens, we'll finally be happy. And I promise—you won't because you'll always set another destination to go for. That's why we need to work to overcome our "Second Cup Addiction" before it drains our happiness.

Here's the interesting truth: research shows that even though people think they will have more time or enhanced enjoyment in the future, the reality is that when the future they've anticipated arrives, they are just as busy and just as likely to put off enjoyment yet again, creating a cyclical pattern of second cup living. Stop postponing your life expecting something better in the future. Live now! When we postpone so much of our happiness for a later date, we waste so many of our precious days.

Of course, we need to plan for our future to get the best outcome possible, but focusing too much on it can really waste a lot of time. Focusing too much of our happiness on future events robs us of savoring each day for the treasure it is. We let so many days pass us by in quest of a more perfect tomorrow. Learn to enjoy each day. By maximizing your present moments on the journey rather than only dreaming about the destination, your daily life becomes richer and more enjoyable.

"It is good to have an end to journey toward; but it is the journey that matters, in the end." Ursula K. Le Guin

So how do we overcome our "Second Cup Addiction" and maximize our present moments? Part of savoring every day is learning to treat each day as a special occasion so that we don't take them for granted. It's easy to find happiness and joy in the big events of our lives—holidays, weddings, graduations, promotions, birthdays, anniversaries, and births. But, it can be more of a struggle to sustain that feeling of joy in the mundane, everyday tasks of our lives. Think of how many days pass us by as we wait on our next holiday gathering, our next vacation, our next birthday, our next raise, our next degree and so forth. So many of us count down the days until our next big event, and we tend to discount those days in between by saying, *"Only 10 days left until…"* If there is nothing special scheduled—no vacation, no holiday, no birthday or anniversary, then the day is considered ordinary and we endure it as if it were some sort of task instead of living it to the fullest.

Learn to find beauty in the ordinary days of life. When you are able to appreciate ordinary, everyday experiences, you are truly savoring today. Make every day special! Why should your good china gather dust in the cupboard until next Christmas? Pull it out and use it for tonight's supper and make an ordinary day feel festive. Burn those beautiful candles that you've been waiting for just the right time to use. Take that vacation you've been putting off. Spend those gift cards you've been saving for just the perfect time. Drink your morning coffee from the favorite tea cup and saucer in your hutch. Use those beautiful dishcloths your best friend embroidered for you. Carry that new purse you bought for just the right occasion.

If you don't choose to embrace and enjoy even life's most ordinary days, you will find yourself passing so much of life by. There really is beauty in making every day more sacred. Don't just wait for the big events to enjoy yourself. The ability to enjoy life in the present is essential. When we learn to enjoy life moment by moment, day by day, we find life becomes more fun and satisfying. Choose to be happy right now. You can find joy in the midst of your everyday life. After all, true life is really not found in arriving at a destination; it's found in the journey.

If you don't start living now, when will you begin? And how will you know it won't be too late? Perhaps this story will touch you as deeply as it did me.

 Second Cup Story: A Story to Live By
By Ann Wells (*Los Angeles Times*)

My brother-in-law opened the bottom drawer of my sister's bureau and lifted out a tissue-wrapped package. *"This,"* he said, *"is not a slip. This is lingerie."* He discarded the tissue and handed me the slip. It was exquisite—silk, handmade, and trimmed with a cobweb of lace. The price tag with an astronomical figure on it was still attached. *"Jan bought this the first time we went to New York, at least 8 or 9 years ago. She never wore it. She was saving it for a special occasion. Well, I guess this is the occasion."*

He took the slip from me and put it on the bed with the other clothes we were taking to the mortician. His hands lingered on the silk material for a moment. Then he slammed the drawer shut and turned to me, *"Don't ever save anything for a special occasion. Every day you're alive is a special occasion."* I remembered those words through the funeral and the days that followed when I helped him and my niece attend to all the sad chores that follow an unexpected death. I thought about them on the plane returning to California from the Midwest where my sister's family lives. I thought about all the things that she hadn't seen or heard or done. I thought about the things that she had done without realizing they were special.

I'm still thinking about his words, and they've changed my life. I'm reading more and dusting less. I'm sitting on the deck and admiring the view without fussing about the weeds in the garden. I'm spending more time with my family and friends and less time in committee meetings. Whenever possible, life should be a pattern of experience to savor, not endure. I'm trying to recognize these moments now and cherish them. I'm not 'saving' anything; we use our good china and crystal for every special event - such as losing a pound, getting the sink unstopped, or the first camellia blossom. I wear my good blazer to the market if I like it. My theory is if I look prosperous, I can shell out $28.49 for one small bag of groceries without wincing. I'm not saving my good perfume for special parties; clerks in hardware stores and tellers in banks have noses that function as well as my party-going friends. *'Someday'* and *'one of these days'* are losing their grip on my vocabulary. If it's worth seeing or hearing or doing, I want to see and hear and do it now.

I'm not sure what my sister would've done had she known that she wouldn't be here for the tomorrow we all take for granted. I think she would have called family members and a few close friends. She might have called a few former friends to apologize and mend fences for past squabbles. I like to think she would have gone out for a Chinese dinner, her favorite food. I'm guessing -I'll never know. It's those little things left undone that would make me angry if I knew that my hours were limited. Angry because I put off seeing good friends whom I was going to get in touch with - someday. Angry because I hadn't written certain letters that I intended to write - one of these days. Angry and sorry that I didn't tell my husband and daughter often enough how much I truly love them.

I'm trying very hard not to put off, hold back, or save anything that would add laughter and luster to our lives. And every morning when I open my eyes, I tell myself that it is special. Every day, every minute, every breath truly is a gift from God.

What are YOU waiting for? If you're thinking you're going to wait until the kids are out of the house, until you're making more money, until your problems aren't so big, or until you can find the time, you may be letting 'good reasons' keep you from enjoying happiness right now. Stop waiting for everything to be 'just right.' Pour yourself into life now! That's a key strategy I want you to take with you from this chapter. Overcome your "Second Cup Addiction" and start to make each day a special occasion.

"Live today. Not yesterday. Not tomorrow. Just today. Inhabit your moments. Don't rent them out to tomorrow. Do you know what you're doing when you spend a moment wondering how things are going to turn out tomorrow? What am I doing? You're cheating yourself out of today. Today is calling to you, trying to get your attention, but you're stuck on tomorrow, and today trickles away like water down a drain. You wake up the next morning and that today you wasted is gone forever. It's now

yesterday. Some of those moments may have had wonderful things in store for you, but now you'll never know." Jerry Spinelli, Author

Grounds for Thought: What in the world are you waiting for before you start focusing on your happiness? Don't you realize your days are numbered? Are you waiting for your real life to begin? What are you waiting to overcome, obtain, or get rid of before experiencing true joy?

Grounds for Action: What things have you been putting off to enjoy until some other day? Start making today a special occasion. I've started enjoying my morning coffee in my favorite porcelain tea cups with their matching saucers—the ones I've had sitting in the hutch (collecting dust) waiting for those 'special' occasions. Well, you know what, I'm a special person and my life IS that special occasion. It's the same reason I've started burning those candles I've been saving for years, using my nice tablecloths on the everyday supper table, buying fresh coffee beans for my morning brew, and picking flowers for the table that I can enjoy. I've learned the importance of making everyday special.

JAVA JOLT #4:
Live Like You're Not Getting Another Cup

"Dream as if you'll live forever. Live as if you'll die today." James Dean, Actor

Whether you realize it or not, everyday above ground is a good day. If you still have breath left in you, you still have the ability to do wonderful things with your life! That means we all need to keep fresh dreams and aspirations in front of us. When our memories are more important to us than our dreams, that's what makes us 'old.' The world is filled with so many women of all ages walking around 'old' that don't even know it. Could you possibly be one of them? Don't allow yourself to become 'old.'

One of the worst feelings than can happen when you reach the end of your life is to realize you never took time to do the things you really wanted or to feel like you wasted your days. Don't risk growing older and having nothing but regrets, wishing you would have pursued the desires in your heart and knowing it's too late. Live a life you can be proud of. Then when you get older and think back, you'll be able to enjoy it a second time! Most importantly, live your days so that when the end of your life comes, you can proudly say, *"Yes, I've lived a great life!"* We can all learn a great lesson from 80-year old Mae.

Second Cup Story:

One day a woman had lunch with friends. Mae, a little lady who was 80-years old came along with them. All the women ordered salads, sandwiches, and soups, except Mae who ordered heated apple pie with two scoops of ice cream.

The other ladies tried to act nonchalant, as if people did this all the time. But when their orders were brought out, they didn't enjoy them. They couldn't take their eyes off Mae as she ate her pie a-la-mode. They ate their lunches silently and frowned.

Finally, one of the ladies asked what everyone was thinking, *"Mae, how come you order rich desserts, while we feel we must be sensible?"*

She laughed and said, *"Because I'm tasting all that is possible."*

She continued: *"I try to eat the food I need, and do the things I should. But life's so short, my friend, I hate missing out on something good. This year I realize how old I was. I haven't been this old before. So before I die, I've got to try those things that for years I had ignored."*

"I haven't smelled all the flowers yet. There are too many books I haven't read. There are more fudge sundaes to wolf down and kites to be flown overhead. There are many malls I haven't shopped. I've not laughed at all the jokes. I've missed a lot of Broadway hits and potato chips and cokes."

"I want to wade again in water and feel ocean spray on my face. I want to sit in a country church once more and thank God for His grace. I want peanut butter every day spread on my morning toast. I want untimed long distance calls to the folks I love the most. I haven't cried at all the movies yet, or walked in the morning rain. I need to feel wind in my hair. I want to fall in love again."

"So if I choose to have dessert, instead of having dinner, then should I die before nightfall, I'd say I died a winner. Because I missed out on nothing. I filled my heart's desire. I had that final pie and ice cream before my life expired."

I encourage you to taste all that is possible for your life! Enjoy every day given to you. Start living like there's no tomorrow. Most of us put our desires and wants on the 'when I have time' list or the 'someday I'd like to' list. Or even worse—some of us don't even have a list of things we still want to accomplish in life. We need to refocus the way we approach life. You have probably heard of a Bucket List—a list of things you want to do before you die. Well, I think we each need to start working on our own Coffee Cup List—things we want to be, do, have or see before our cup runs dry. Try to accomplish some each year and check them off your list. Live well during the time you are here so that when the time comes you don't get another cup, you'll have no regrets! Make these next years your best years. Stop saving the best for last; save the best for *now*.

"Life is not measured by the number of breaths we take, but by the number of moments that take our breath away." Unknown

I recently heard about a new challenge called the 'One Month to Live Challenge.' A husband and wife wrote a book and are encouraging their readers to live the next 30 days like it was their last. The results have been powerful. When people face their own mortality they start to live life moment-by-moment and more whole-heartedly. When time is limited, you learn to live a no-regrets life. The truth is, you have no idea how much time is in front of you versus how much time you've already used up. For all you and I know, these next 30 days could be our last. Being unaware of our remaining time is a *good* thing. The mere notion that we don't know if we have 20 years, 20 days or 20 seconds, should make us savor each day more fully.

None of us is guaranteed a tomorrow. Whether you are 29 or 92, you could have the same amount of time remaining on this earth. It's time to make the most of the time you've got left. The positive changes you've been thinking about making 'someday' or those dreams you've been meaning to get to 'someday' need to be done. Don't put off making worthwhile changes because you expect or anticipate that you have a certain amount of time remaining. This type of procrastination could end with a too little, too late result. Stop living like you've got all the time in the world.

Suppose you knew that this was your last year on earth. What would you do with your days? How would you spend the remaining time? Are there dreams and desires you would regret leaving undone? Answer that and you will have answered how you ought to live every day. Wouldn't you want to pack it full of the greatest experiences—of love, friendship, dreams, joys—everything good? The date of our last cup is likely not going to be something we can adequately prepare for in advance. It's doubtful we'll receive the notification that we're on our 'last refill' and allow us adequate opportunity to change the way we've been living. Realize you aren't guaranteed another cup so you'd better start savoring today. Start living each day as if it's your last, not because you're going to die, but because you're going to live much more fully!

Grounds for Thought: When your cup runs dry, how fully will you be able to say you lived your life? Are you living or just existing? Are there things you are talking about but not doing? If you knew you only had one month to live, what would you regret not doing? If this were your last day on earth, would you be happy with how you've spent your time today, this week, or this year? Feel good about the priorities you're focused on at this point in your life? Feel complete and at peace with the people who matter most?

Grounds for Action: It's time to make *your* Coffee Cup list. Write out a list of 25 things you want to be, do, have, or see before your cup runs dry. Don't let your life slip through your fingers with regrets. Instead, learn to delight in the days you are given. Download a Coffee Cup List at: www.theinspirationalcoffeeclub.com.

The Last Cup

It may sound cliché, but today is the only time you have. It's too late for yesterday and you can't depend on tomorrow, so you need to learn to savor today. Don't throw away today worrying about tomorrow or regretting yesterday. Whatever happened yesterday, last week, or last year and whatever's going on tomorrow, next week, or next month are not nearly as important as how you choose to live today. Start living your days to the fullest. Each day is unique and irreplaceable. Once each day is gone, you can never get it back.

You're getting older every day. Learn to live each day as if this were the last one you will have—for it could be; you just never know. Our days are not promised. Today is the only sure thing. Don't move so fast that you don't take time to savor each day. Take life one day at a time. There's great enjoyment to be had. Don't you dare miss it!

Life is indeed too short and too precious to race through too quickly. The sad fact is that there are many people who exist but do not live. Remember, this is the only life you get. This is not a dress rehearsal with any do-over's; this is the real deal. How you decide to live it is up to you. Slow down and savor what each day has to offer. We don't get to choose how long we are here on earth, but we do get to decide what to do with the time that is given to us. It is our decision. When you die, what matters most isn't the date you were born or the date that you died. It's the time between those years that matters most. How did you live? Remember to live fully! Take advantage of this opportunity called life.

My hope for you is that you have the rest of your life to look forward to, but most importantly, you learn to focus on the rest of today first. Make the best of every moment. Who's to say you'll ever have that opportunity again? Don't wait; start enjoying life today! Remember, everyday is a gift from God so get up each day and give it your best for none of us is guaranteed another cup.

"This is the day that the Lord has made, let us rejoice and be glad in it!" Psalm 118:24

GROUND RULE #8

Take Time to Fill Another's Cup ~ Make a Difference

"To the world you may only be one person, but to one person, you may be the world."
Unknown

Filling Another's Cup Fills Your Life With Joy

"It is one of the most beautiful compensations in life…that no man can sincerely try to help another without helping himself." Ralph Waldo Emerson

We weren't created to live for ourselves. We were created to add value to the lives of others. On our journey to fill our own cups, we must also be on the look-out for ways we can pour happiness onto those around us. People tend to feel better about their own lives when they know they are making a difference in someone else's. Happiness is a natural result of doing something to make someone else happy. What you pour into the lives of others can't help but come back into your own, often causing you to overflow with joy. This is why filling another's cup is one of the surest ways of adding fulfillment to our lives.

"In helping others, we shall help ourselves, for whatever good we give out completes the circle and comes back to us." Flora Edwards

Amidst our busy lives, it's easy to get caught up in our own little world and focus only on ourselves. When we get too focused on our own lives, we lose so much of the richness we most desire. It is by reaching out and connecting with those around us that our hearts are filled with happiness. However, we need to purposely seek out ways to make a difference each day. Otherwise, it's too easy to rush through life and miss the opportunities all around us.

The world is so big that's it's easy to wonder, *What can I do that will possibly make a difference?* Trust me, you can make far more impact than you ever imagined. You can make a big difference with even the smallest actions. No one is insignificant and no act of kindness too small. In fact, your kindness may make all the difference in the world to someone. Let me use this famous story to illustrate.

**Second Cup Story:**
Early one morning as a Grandfather and his grandson were walking along the beach they came across a starfish that had washed up on the

shore during high tide.

The grandson reached down and gently picked up the starfish, still moist and alive. *"It's beautiful, Grandpa, what's going to happen to it?"* the boy asked.

The grandfather replied that the starfish would eventually die. Sensing his grandson's sadness, he quickly explained it was okay because the starfish would become a source of food for other sea creatures. He told the boy that he should not be sad because it is all part of the cycle of life.

A few minutes later, the grandfather sat down to read his newspaper and enjoy his morning coffee. After awhile, he noticed his grandson had wandered back down to the beach. He called out, *"Son, what are you doing?"*

The young boy paused, looked up, and replied, *"Throwing the starfish back into the ocean."*

"I can see that," the grandfather responded. *"I guess I should have asked, why are you throwing the starfish in the ocean?"*

"The sun is up and the tide is going out. And if I don't throw them in they'll die."

"Oh, son, don't you realize there are miles and miles of beach and starfish all along it. You can't possibly make a difference!"

With childlike innocence the grandson bent down, picked up another starfish and threw it into the ocean. The young boy said, *"To that one, Grandpa, I just made all the difference."*

No matter how small or insignificant it may be, an act of kindness is never wasted. You may never fully realize the impact your actions make on those around you. There is something very special in each and every one of us. We have all been gifted with the ability to make a difference, and if we can become aware of that gift, we can transform our lives along with others. Opportunities to make a difference are all around us. If you make it a regular goal to find ways to add more value to other people, you will never have to worry about fulfillment.

Ultimately, what shapes the meaning of our life is not what we get but what we give. Use your life to touch others. If each day you can sincerely feel like you've given something of value to those around you, I can promise you'll experience the ultimate victory of life—a life of meaning and joy.

Each of us has within us the power to make a lasting impact on the lives of others. Remember, we are here to lift each other up and to help as best we can, whenever we can. The more we do just that, the more our lives overflow with happiness. Let me give you some ideas on how to fill another's cup.

Grounds for Thought: Do you feel like you make a difference? How do you feel when you know you're filling someone else's cup? How is someone's life better because they crossed your path? Are you remembering to serve others while caring for your own needs?

JAVA JOLT #1:
Refill the Cups of Those Who Have Filled Yours

"Never worry about numbers. Help one person at a time, and always start with the person nearest you." Mother Teresa

Throughout our lives we encounter people who help shape us into the person we are today. Think of those individuals who have made us feel appreciated and special, or we have depended on during difficult challenges, or who have mentored us, loved us, and encouraged us. We often remember their kind words and gestures for years to come, but all too often, those people don't have any idea of the impact they have had on our lives. The people we often find most difficult to acknowledge are the ones closest to us. However, if there's anyone whose cups we should fill, it should be those who have helped us along our journey through life. Making a difference should start by filling the cups of those who have filled yours.

"There is more hunger for love and appreciation in this world than for bread." Mother Teresa

Typically the people closest to us get overlooked when it comes time for appreciation and recognition. How many times has someone close to you really made a difference in your life, but you've struggled to show them how much they mean to you? Maybe a parent, grandparent, spouse, sibling, child, teacher, friend, aunt, or boss? Unfortunately, most of us wait until a person is gone before we tell them how much they meant to us and then our opportunity is gone. Don't let this happen to you. Tell the people who have helped, loved, and encouraged you most they are special and important to you before it's too late. Let those who have made a difference in your life know how much they impacted you. Fill other people's cups while they are still able to enjoy it.

I think one of the most valuable ways to fill the cups of those closest to us is to put your feelings in a handwritten note. People cherish handwritten notes for years. If you're like me, you've kept every one of those precious notes you've ever received. I call these little notes "Creamers" because they add so much flavor and richness to life. When you express heartfelt sentiments in letters to those who have encouraged you, supported you, sacrificed for you, and mentored you, you'll be surprised at how positively moving this will be for the recipient as well as for you. People love being appreciated by someone. Your cup gets filled right along with the person's cup you are filling. In fact, the giver always receives more than the receiver. Take some time to send some "Creamers" to those who have made and continue to make a difference in your life.

Ever hung up the phone or got done visiting with someone and thought, *I am so lucky to have that person in my life?* Why not write them a quick note to let them know that? When's the last time you told someone how much you appreciated their presence in your life? Too often we spend more time expressing our frustrations and disappointments with the ones closest to us than we do acknowledging what we really appreciate about them. It's time to start letting more people around you know just how much they mean to you.

It's true that the majority of us don't get enough praise, but it's also a fact that we usually don't give others enough praise either. Can you remember the last time you praised someone? Filling others' cups builds and strengthens bonds with people. You'll have better friendships, marriages, and working relationships. Plus, you'll be healthier, happier, and on your way to a more fulfilling life. Take every opportunity to increase the positive emotions of those around you. Filling another's cup starts with reinforcing the relationships that have impacted you most in life.

"You cannot do a kindness too soon, for you never know how soon it will be too late."
Ralph Waldo Emerson

You may never fully realize the impact your words of appreciation could leave on someone. Let this true story be an example.

 **Second Cup Story:**

At a speaking engagement, an inspirational speaker asked the audience to think deeply of someone who had really impacted them throughout their life and to write a thank-you note to that person. One of the men in the audience thought of his 8th grade literature teacher because she was always a favorite teacher, and students still talked about her at class reunions. It took him nearly two months to track his teacher down, but he eventually found her and wrote her a short note.

The following week he received a letter back from her. It read, *Dear John, You will never know how much your letter meant to me. I am 83-years old and I am living all alone in one room. My friends are all gone. My family's gone. I taught for 50 years and yours is the first thank you letter I have ever gotten from a student. Sometimes I wonder what I did with my life. I will read and re-read your letter until the day I die.*

This teacher had always been a favorite at the school. Everyone loved her, but no one had ever told her.

Let this be a reminder of just how important it is to let people know how much they mean to us. Don't assume that other people are thanking those around us. If we don't tell them, they may never know. We all want to feel appreciated. We all want to know our life has had significance. It is such a blessing to receive notes of thanks. Those who receive them treasure them for years. It only takes one person to change one life. That one person may be you.

Taking time to acknowledge and appreciate someone who has impacted us is a great way to make a difference. This simple act of kindness bonds people together in a very powerful way that can shift a relationship forever. There are many ways to thank someone for filling your cup, but I think sending a little note—adding a little "Creamer" in their cup—is one of the easiest, most effective actions you can take. If you've been blessed by someone, let them now be blessed by you. Start by acknowledging your parents, children, spouse, family, friends, co-workers, and mentors. Whose cup can you fill this week?

Grounds for Thought: What is the nicest thing anyone's done for you? Who do you need to appreciate more? Is there someone who has made a difference in your life that you have not properly thanked?

Grounds for Action: Thank someone who has filled your cup. Make a list of all the people who have contributed in a positive way to your life and whose impact you still remember today from teachers to coaches to bosses to children to relatives to neighbors to church leaders. Who has helped you become the person you are today—a parent, grandparent, aunt or sibling who made you feel loved and accepted, an employer or teacher who believed in and encouraged your potential, friends who have helped you through a difficult time, family who has made you feel appreciated and special, someone who has inspired you or believed in you when you doubted yourself? Anyone who has contributed to your life deserves positive words from you.

Make it a habit of starting to send more "Creamers" to fill others up. Pick one person each week and write them a short note telling them what qualities and strengths you most appreciate. Written recognition is important because it gives lasting acknowledgment—something the recipient can reflect on over and over. Take every opportunity to increase the positive emotions of those around you.

Extra Jolt Challenge: If there's a person who is really close to you that you want to thank even a little extra for filling your cup, here's a fantastic idea. Find a pretty mug or tea cup, and fill it with folded sheets of colored paper that list things you love, admire, or appreciate about them (values they taught, happy memories shared, encouragement they gave, what you love about them). You can also throw in some inspirational sayings. I guarantee they will treasure your wonderful gesture.

"At times our own light goes out and is rekindled by a spark from another person. Each of us has cause to thank with deep gratitude of those who have lighted the flame within us." Albert Schwietzer

JAVA JOLT #2:
Pour Encouragement Onto Those Around You

"Kind words can be short and easy to speak, but their echoes are truly endless."
Mother Teresa

You and I have an assignment: everywhere we go, we should be encouraging others—building them up, challenging them to reach for new heights and helping them to succeed. There isn't one person who doesn't get discouraged in this journey of life. *Everyone* you know needs encouragement. So be on the lookout for people you can uplift. Every day we can make such an impact by pouring encouragement onto those around us.

It's easy to nitpick and find fault with others, but if you really want to make a difference, your goal needs to be to build others up. Make sure that you are bringing out the best in all those around you. When people are around us, we should leave them feeling better off than they were previously. Here's proof of how a little encouragement makes a big difference.

 **Second Cup Story:**

A man opened the front door of his house one morning to get his newspaper and the little dog that lived across the street was enthusiastically bringing his paper to him. The man chuckled, hurried back inside, and got the dog a treat to reward his great effort. That little dog left there just as happy as could be. The next morning when the man opened the door to pick up his newspaper again, that same little dog was sitting there by the door, and next to the dog was not one, but eight of the neighbors' newspapers!

Humans respond similarly to treats—especially when we are treated with praise and encouragement. Learn not to take others for granted, especially those closest to you (your family, friends, and co-workers). One of the most valuable ways to make a difference in someone's life is to build others up as often as you can. It's amazing what a kind word can do. When's the last time you said, *"I think you're great." "I'm so glad you're my mom." "You are the best husband." "You're doing a wonderful job." "I'm so proud of you."* When you start encouraging others, you will draw out the good in them. They will start treating you differently as well. Help those closest to you feel strong, confident, and secure.

Whether we realize it or not, one of the most significant ways to make a difference is by helping others become all they can be—our children, our friends, our spouses, and people around us. Get in the habit of complimenting others. *"You did great on your project." "You look beautiful." "What a great meal." "You provided such great service."* Verbalize your thoughts. You can think great thoughts about someone, but it won't do them any good until you speak them out loud. Build up anyone from your friends to your boss to the daycare worker to the waitress to the cashier at the grocery checkout.

"Therefore encourage one another and build up one another..." 1 Thessalonians 5:11

I believe every day we meet someone we can encourage with a kind word. Start to look for the best qualities in everyone you come into contact with. Everybody needs somebody, and that somebody could be you. Encouragement turns lives around; it changes people, and it makes people better. It really allows people to make turning points in their lives. Here's a true story that's living proof of the power of encouragement.

Second Cup Story:

Throughout his youth, Bob Danzig was in five foster homes. When he was nine-years old and being moved to yet another foster home, his social worker sat him down, looked him straight in the eyes and said, *"Bobby, I want you to always remember these words: you are worthwhile."* Those words took Bob by surprise. No one had ever said anything like that to him before. Those words stuck with him.

When he got older, Bob took a job at the New York Times as copy boy. A few months into his job, his first boss called him into her office, and he thought he was being fired. She said, *"Bob, I have been watching you and I believe you are full of promise."* Those words, on that day, gave him permission to aspire.

Those two positive messages played over and over in his head. Years later, he became CEO of Hearst Newspapers, one of the largest newspaper companies in the world. He credits it all to those simple words of appreciation and love. What a wonderful example of how little words of encouragement can make such a difference!

Opportunities to encourage others are all around us. Recently I was at my dentist office, and a new hygienist was cleaning my teeth. She did a great job, and I told her so as I was leaving. She got a big smile, and said, *"Really? Thanks. I've been doubting myself."* I can still see that smile that spread across her face. My few simple words of encouragement could be just what helps keep her going.

Keep your eyes open for ways to encourage others daily. Help others feel better about themselves. Mentor others. Believe in others. Invest in others. Make others feel important and appreciated. Praise others when they are trying to better themselves. If you meet someone who is doing a great job, tell them. If you meet someone you believe has incredible promise and talent, let them know. If you admire certain qualities about a person, be sure to share them. Make a difference with words of encouragement wherever you are. When you leave a person feeling good about themselves, you feel *great* about yourself.

Our society overflows with faultfinders. So be a person who builds others up, not tears them down. The world needs more people to speak into the hearts of others and say, "*I believe in you." "Follow your dream." "Keep it up." "You have great potential."* We hold a special place in our hearts for those who encourage us. I challenge you to be an encourager. Lift someone up who is feeling down, believe in someone who is taking a chance, and help people see what is possible instead of impossible. In doing so, you are filling another's cup. Your words have the power to change someone's life. Use them daily to make a difference to those you come in contact with.

"The greatest gift you can do for another is not share your riches, but reveal to him his own." Benjamin Disraley

Grounds for Thought: Can you think of a time when you have been on the receiving end of positive and encouraging words? How did they make you feel? Are you encouraging those around you: your children, spouse, co-workers, and friends? Is there someone you see great potential in that you can encourage? Is there someone you've been lovingly holding back by being that 'realist' in their lives? Have you encouraged your spouse and kids lately?

Grounds for Action: Encourage at least one person each day. Ask yourself daily, *"Who did I encourage today?"* Somebody needs your support. Look for and recognize the good in others.

JAVA JOLT #3:
"Pour It Forward" With Random Acts of Kindness

"Those who bring sunshine to the lives of others cannot keep it from themselves."
James Barrie

One of my favorite ways to fill a person's cup is to do something nice unexpectedly—I call this "Pouring it Forward." Random acts of kindness have that certain element of surprise that adds to the pleasure of the gesture—both for the giver and the recipient. And little acts of kindness can change the world more than you can ever imagine. I think of the times I've received an unexpected note in the mail or a sack of vegetables from the neighbor hanging on my doorknob or a loaf of homemade banana bread from a loved one. The smallest actions can take you by surprise and completely make your day, sometimes even change a life!

When you share your kindness randomly, you may never really know the effect your actions will have. But I can guarantee you this—the power of simple acts of kindness is stronger than any jolt of caffeine. What you put into the lives of others comes back in your own and then some. Each time you pour kind and generous acts forward to others, your own reservoirs are filled again. It's not the things you get but the hearts you touch that will determine your success in life.

Random acts of kindness don't have to be big to be effective. A lot of little things can make a big difference! Mother Teresa said, *"Small deeds done with great love do great good."* Look for opportunities to give small, unexpected gifts to others. When you do things unexpectedly you will get greater joy. There is an array of small kindness opportunities that present themselves daily and could be extremely meaningful to those around you.

"Remember there's no such thing as a small act of kindness. Every act creates a ripple with no logical end." Scott Adams

Every encounter with another person is an opportunity to provide an act of kindness whether we realize it or not. When we start to think this way, it becomes easier to reach out. It's little actions that have the potential to add up to big things. The possibilities for random acts of kindness exist all around you—you simply have to open your eyes, open your mouth, and most importantly, open your heart. One morning I was waiting for my dad while he was at a doctor's appointment. So I decided to go get a cup of coffee from the complimentary pot in the lobby. I noticed an elderly lady sitting a few chairs down from me so I asked her if she'd like me to grab her a cup of coffee as well. She seemed so surprised that I had even asked. So I got us both a cup and when I was leaving with my dad, she grabbed my hand and said, *"Thank you so much. You made a difference to me."* A simple cup of free hospital coffee did that—proof that random acts of kindness do not have to be big or expensive to make an impact! It's amazing how one little act can brighten someone's day.

Be on the lookout for opportunities to do good. You can't sit back and wait for opportunities to come to you. Take time to care. Take time to meet other people's needs. Leave unexpected deposits of kindness wherever you go. It's the small, daily differences that make an impact.

To "Pour it Forward" you could leave some cash in an envelope for a struggling co-worker, make coffee for the office, set treats out on the table, buy a cup of coffee for the person in line behind you, deposit coins into a person's expired parking meter, send a gift card to someone, make a handmade blanket for a cancer patient, visit an elderly neighbor living alone, bake goodies for someone, pray for someone, be a mentor, watch a friend's children so she can do something for herself, let a stranger into traffic on a busy street, leave a little extra tip for the waitress at the local restaurant, donate the clothes you no longer wear, write a letter to a military hero, give someone fresh flowers or produce from your garden, shovel a neighbor's sidewalk, volunteer at your favorite charity, sponsor a child through church, offer a home-cooked meal to someone hurting, participate in a walk-for-a-cause, cook Thanksgiving dinner for someone all alone, drive an elderly person to church, drop off homemade goodies to a local homeless shelter, let the person behind you have the front row parking spot at the grocery store, befriend a stranger, and on and on and on.

A cup somewhere is waiting to be filled! Don't waste another moment. Each morning, wake up and say, *"What good can I do today?"* When you go to bed, ask, *"What good did I do today?"* I challenge you to find one small way to make the world a little better today. Make at least one person smile each day. If we all do that, we have created a movement of love and joy. A new study suggests that the feeling of gratitude someone experiences after being on the receiving end of an act of kindness can lead to greater social good as those recipients are more likely to give back—and not only to the person who helped them. One act of kindness leads to another, and another, and another. They will add up to something big in the life of another. And before you know it, we can change the world with a small act. Be a part of the "Pour it Forward" movement today!

Grounds for Thought: Do you remember the last random act of kindness someone did for you? How did it make you feel? How openly have you been sharing your time, talents, and treasures to make a difference for others? When was the last time you offered a kind gesture out of the blue?

Grounds for Action: Each day, find someone to be a blessing to. Make it a goal to do something good unexpectedly for one person every day. Before you go to bed each evening, ask yourself, *"What good did I do today?"*

The Last Cup

You may not see yourself as a woman of influence, but I believe you are *always* making a difference, every day, and in every moment. As soon as you wake up each morning, you become the cause of a series of ripple effects that will forever affect the direction and experience of many lives around you—from your children and spouse to your co-workers to the attendant at the drive-thru window to your customers to your neighbors. Each one of us has the power within us to make a difference for others. We should seek out ways to help, even small ways, whenever we can and remember to start with those closest to you. One person can make a difference. Small acts of kindness have the potential to add up to something bigger in the life of another. How many others have been blessed by you?

Taking time to fill another person's cup provides a sense of satisfaction in life that few other experiences can top. It is in giving that we receive the greatest gift. When we extend ourselves to others we not only fill the cup of another, but it ends up that we are also refilled and refreshed. Slowly but surely, you'll notice that the positive energy you're putting out comes back to you. If you make someone else's life happy, your life is filled with joy.

Don't miss any opportunity to do good. Give more than you ever expect to receive, look for ways to add value to others, and bring joy to those you meet. When you make a contribution to others' lives, it helps you realize how much your own life matters. Fill as many cups as possible on your journey to filling yours. Ask yourself each day, *"What did I do today to make someone's life a little sweeter?"*

Rather than trying to figure out what everybody can do for you, start looking for things that you can do for someone else. Fill cups wherever you go. As you do so, your life will be filled with so much enjoyment. If you make someone else happy, you will be happy. The best way to be fulfilled is to get your mind off yourself and reach out to others!

"The time to be happy is now. The place to be happy is here. The way to be happy is to make others so." Robert G. Ingersoll

GROUND RULE #9

Leave Room for Cream and Sugar ~ Enjoy Yourself

"And in the end it's not the years in your life that count. It's the life in your years."
Abraham Lincoln

Life Tastes Better When Sweetened With Fun

"You don't stop laughing because you grow old. You grow old because you stop laughing." Michael Pritchard

For some reason, as we grow older we seem to repress our sense of fun in preference for something called 'maturity.' It becomes so easy to take life too seriously or become so wrapped up in our day-to-day routines that sometimes we forget to leave time for some plain old fun. Many adults have a dreadfully low fun factor which is so sad because life tastes best when sweetened with fun! It's time you relearn how to mix a little more enjoyment and fun—what I call cream and sugar—into your everyday life again.

Fun is a vital requirement for a high-quality life, yet it's often the one that gets shorted. Sure, you can drink your coffee black, but it's far more enjoyable and tasty when you add a little cream and sugar. Life is no different. Much like we have to add our own cream and sugar to make the taste of our coffee more desirable, we also have to add our own cream and sugar moments to our lives to make them more enjoyable.

You were created for both work *and* play. Fun and laughter is what helps bring restoration to your soul. So stop taking yourself so seriously. When you take a light-hearted approach to life, you become a more enjoyable person to be around and life naturally feels happier. Times of pure enjoyment are not just recreation; they are what allow us to delight in our lives. The great thing is that pleasurable cream and sugar moments are all around us and can easily be added to life.

"Ask not what fun does for you. Ask rather what you do for fun." Unknown

Take regular time to indulge yourself in pure enjoyment. You can and deserve to enjoy your life journey, but it's up to you to make that happen. You must be responsible to do whatever it takes to add laughter and joy. Give yourself a dose of fun on a regular basis. Life's cream and sugar moments are what living is all about. Add some to your life each and every day. Let me show you some simple ways to add a bit of pure enjoyment back into your life.

Grounds for Thought: Are you taking life too seriously? Can you say you're having just as much fun as you grow older? Do you look at people having fun with resentment wishing that was you? On a scale from one to ten, how would you rate your fun factor? What are some of the most fun times you've ever had? How often do you take time to simply enjoy yourself?

JAVA JOLT #1:
Laughter is a Calorie-Free Sweetener

"The most wasted of all days is one without laughter." E.E. Cummings

Laughter is one of the most fulfilling simple pleasures, but one that many of us have lost. In the midst of our hectic lives, it's easy to become so serious that we lose touch with the laughter inside us which then begins to decrease our overall sense of well-being. Did you know the average child laughs an average of 113 times per day? But by the time we're adults, we only laugh an average of four to eight times a day. A recent study says we need at least 12 laughs a day just to stay healthy. How many times have you laughed today?

Laughter should be a part of your daily routine. It's good for your health. You've heard the phrase, *'Laughter is the best medicine.'* Now there's actually research that shows that laughter *is* good medicine for life. Ever notice that after a good, hard laugh you feel renewed energy and joy? That's because laughter causes your brain to release endorphins that create a positive state of mind and boost optimism, self-confidence, and feelings of self-worth. So naturally, it leaves you with an improved attitude. Further, laughter is a natural stress reducer. Evidence also shows that laughter can boost the immune system as well as decrease your chances of a heart attack. When you laugh, you become healthier. Laugh longer and live longer!

"Joyfulness keeps the heart and face young. A good laugh makes us better friends with ourselves and everybody around us." Orison Swett Marden

You have a choice—you can allow yourself to become uptight and serious about life or you can lighten up, and realize that even on days when nothing seems to be going right, laughter allows you to get through anything. Fulfillment increases when we can learn to laugh even in the midst of difficult situations. Laugh at yourself, laugh with others, and do it easily and often. Laughter is the best pick-me-up.

Make it a habit to hang around fun people. We need people in our life who make us laugh and unleash our inner comedian. Spend lots of time with the people and things that make you laugh the most. I know God has a sense of humor; he sent me a man who's *not* a coffee drinker but who is one of the funniest people I know. For that, I'll overlook the non-coffee drinking quality.

"Laughter is your heart's way of telling your face to smile." D. Green

Identify the things that make you feel light, happy, and fun. Read funny emails and jokes, go to the store and read funny greeting cards, and spend lots of time with friends who make you laugh. Do you have favorite sitcoms or movies that always make you chuckle? One of my all-time favorite shows is *'The Golden Girls.'* There isn't a single episode I watch that doesn't make me laugh numerous times. Find a show or movie that makes you chuckle out loud and give yourself permission to watch a rerun once in awhile. Better yet, watch that show with a person who makes you laugh and get double the enjoyment. I even heard there are Laughter Clubs popping up around the nation for the sheer goal of helping people laugh more.

Laughter is good for your soul! It helps balance out the seriousness of life. A sense of humor, especially laughing at yourself, can be one of life's greatest blessings. Have you been taking yourself too seriously?

Grounds for Thought: On average, how many times do you laugh each day? Are you taking yourself and your life too seriously?

When's the last time you laughed so hard your stomach hurt? Have you learned to laugh at yourself?

Grounds for Action: Keep track of the number of times you laugh out loud today. Give yourself a dose of laughter. Watch a funny movie, read funny jokes, or call a friend who always makes you laugh. Make a list of people, shows, and things that make you laugh. Spend some time daily around those things.

JAVA JOLT #2:
Unleash Your Inner Child (and don't worry, coffee won't stunt its growth!)

"I think of life itself now as a wonderful play that I've written for myself, and so my purpose is to have the utmost fun playing my part." Shirley MacLaine

We were never intended to grow up into the kind of serious adults most of us have become. We are intended to remain in many ways childlike. Of course, it's important for us to grow up, but that doesn't mean we should lose our playfulness. Most of us let work, chores, activities, and tasks become more important than play. When you start to take yourself too seriously, you start to miss out on so much of life's enjoyment. Unleashing your inner child is another way to add back in some of the fun you may have lost in your life.

As grown-ups we forget that the simple pleasures we enjoyed as children are still all around us, there for the taking. And most of those are free, right in our own backyards or homes. Sometimes we just need to disconnect from our everyday lives and tap into our inner child where some of our greatest pleasures of our life occur. There is something magical that takes place when we revert back to the activities we enjoyed as kids. You may find that what really makes you happy could be something much more basic than you imagined. Take time to recapture some of your childhood pleasures. Don't get so focused on just getting everything done each day that you neglect the pure delight of play.

As we grow older, we need more childish moments to balance out our seriousness. You need the kind of carefree moments that you enjoyed as a child while having only one goal in mind—fun! How quickly we lose the pleasures of childhood. The happiest women are the ones who remember to hold on to their childhood spontaneity. Something interesting I've noticed as I get older is that it takes courage to play in a world that doesn't play. Others may look at us like we're the odd ones somehow. But where does it say life has to be taken so seriously? In fact, the word 'silly' is derived from a Greek word that means 'blessed.' So there is something sacred in being able to be silly.

Sure, we can't go back to those carefree days of childhood, but we can recapture a few stolen moments from our youth to remind us how precious they were. When you recreate that childhood state of uninhibited joy, you actually create new kinds of happiness. We do ourselves a favor when we learn to play again.

"It is a happy talent to know how to play." Ralph Waldo Emerson

Here are some ideas to unleash your inner child and incorporate the valuable qualities of playfulness into adulthood: play in the leaves, run barefoot in the grass, fly a kite, pick a bouquet of dandelions in your yard, go 'camping' in the backyard, play a fun childhood board game, blow bubbles, twirl or skip, dance in your living room to your favorite song, ride your bike, hula hoop, run through a sprinkler, gather a group of friends and play Candy Land, Twister, Old Maid or musical chairs, squish a mud pie, play hopscotch on the sidewalk, throw yourself a tea party, go swinging or teeter-tottering at the park, watch for falling stars and make a wish, jump on your mattress, dress up your pet, lay on your back and watch the clouds float by, look for the Big Dipper, visit the zoo, ride the go-carts, track down the ice cream truck and buy your favorite treat, make a snow angel or snowman, go sledding, chase a hot air balloon, feed the ducks at the park, eat watermelon outside and see how far you can spit the seeds, watch fireflies and catch them in a jar, watch Saturday morning cartoons while eating breakfast in bed, play your old instrument, decorate sugar cookies, carve or paint a pumpkin, catch snowflakes with your tongue, look for the man in the moon, hold a slumber party with your favorite friends, buy new crayons and color, throw a childhood birthday party with hats, horns, and goodie bags, and many, many more!

Each one of has a suppressed inner child waiting for permission to come out and play. Childhood activities bring back a sense of fun, laughter and wonder that we should never let slip away. No matter how busy or how old you are, try to find a way back to the playfulness and humor you've shared in the past. Regularly take time to capture a few stolen moments from your childhood and see what kind of enjoyment it brings. Have fun and play often. It can't help but make you feel happy.

Grounds for Thought: When is the last time you did something silly? Have you forgotten how to play? Do you remember the last time you unleashed your inner child? What were your favorite activities as a kid?

Grounds for Action: Act like a kid this week! Pick one action from above and do it. If you don't want to act silly alone, grab your funniest friend and do something childlike together.

JAVA JOLT #3:
Simple Pleasures Can Be Some of the Sweetest Treasures

"Enjoy the little things, for one day you make look back and realize they were the big things." Robert Brault

Things do not have to be big, exotic, expensive, or complicated to be enjoyable. In fact, life's simplest pleasures can be some of life's sweetest treasures. I actually find myself happier on those days when I make a point of savoring simple pleasures like enjoying my coffee on my deck where I can listen to the birds in the morning or notice how beautiful my flowers look as the sun is rising in the distance.

Of course, you have to actually *see* the flowers first. It sounds cliché, but you truly need to learn to stop and smell the flowers. Most of us rush through our days, unaware of what goes on around us, missing some of life's most pleasurable moments. We allow ourselves to get distracted by our to-do list instead of enjoying the beauty around us. Think of how many times you have been driving and missed a gorgeous sunrise or sunset in the distance or a rainbow in the sky after a rain, or the daily growth of new leaves in the spring.

One of the saddest things about growing up is how easy it is to miss these things when we're hustling through life. We've gotten so busy that we've forgotten how to enjoy simple, everyday things. Simple pleasures are all around us, just waiting to be enjoyed, explored, and appreciated. Most of them involve nature, friends, family, and pets. When was the last time you watched the sun rise or set, saw the fluffy clouds pass, enjoyed the fireflies in your backyard, watched for falling stars, enjoyed a full moon, listened to the crickets, watched the birds in your feeder and butterflies on your flowers, enjoyed the smell of a refreshing, soaking rain and then delighted in a bright, beautiful rainbow, or enjoyed the flowers in your garden? Have you ever really noticed the change of the seasons with the colorful fall leaves or the first snowfall glistening on the branches? God's creation is magnificent. Start paying more attention to life's natural beauty. Simple pleasures are all around us, just waiting to be enjoyed, explored, and appreciated. There is something truly amazing about these kinds of simple pleasures. Their rejuvenating ability is just awesome.

"Life's greatest pleasures are life's simple treasures." Unknown

Enjoying yourself comes from learning to find the joy in everyday things that we take for granted. Start seeing everyday things in new ways. You have everything you need to enjoy your life just as it is, but you must be responsible for recognizing it and using those cream and sugar moments to add joy to your life. Delightful moments are all around us from the delicious aroma of a new flavored coffee, sitting by the fireplace with a good book, cuddling in your favorite fleece pajamas, listening to your cat purr, lighting a new delicious-smelling candle, or eating a homemade caramel roll fresh from the oven! Be on the lookout for the enjoyment in mundane, everyday experiences. You won't find it if you are barreling through life. By choosing to find the beauty and magnificence in every moment, you'll begin to experience a whole new kind of enjoyment.

Happiness consists more in the small pleasures that occur every day than the larger events. These fleeting times, when added together, equate to a life well-lived! Someday you'll look back and realize the little things were the big things. So choose to look for the beauty in everyday experiences.

Grounds for Thought: What are some of your favorite simple pleasures? Have you forgotten how to enjoy the everyday joys? Do you remember the last time you simply stopped to smell the flowers? Do you need to slow down and stop taking these things for granted?

Grounds for Action: Turn off the television, put down your cell phone, pull yourself away from the computer, and spend time enjoying life's simple pleasures surrounding you. When you start "opening" your eyes, you'll find that cream and sugar moments can be found in the most ordinary of places. Take a 10-minute walk to watch the sunset or sit quietly on your deck in the evening and watch for fireflies or falling stars or take a blanket to the park and lay on the grass, immersing yourself in the beauty of nature that surrounds you. Solely focus on the simple pleasures around you—the sights, smells, and sounds. When we make time for them, these simple joys can add so much sweetness to life.

JAVA JOLT #4:
Girlfriends Are Like Sugar Cubes in the Cup of Life

"A friend is a gift you give yourself." Robert Louis Stevenson

The way I see it, good friends and good coffee are two of life's greatest perks! If you ever feel guilty about spending time with your girlfriends, there's no reason to. This time is essential for our emotional and mental health. Time with girlfriends can restore our sanity, bring us back to our best self and remind us that having fun is a good thing! (And the memories are sure to be among the best moments of your life.) Time spent with other women is more than just fun—it's vital. In the coffee cup of life, friends are the sugar cubes. If you want to taste the sweetest enjoyment life has to offer, start spending more time with your girlfriends. Having fun with friends is like adding extra sugar to your coffee (but without all the added calories!)

Here's the problem: every time we get too busy with work and family the first thing we do is let go of our friendships with other women. When's the last time you got together with your girlfriends, and it didn't involve birthday parties, business meetings, jewelry parties and such? It can be very difficult to keep the same close ties we've had. The bonds of female friendship can easily become lost when we combine work, managing households, and raising families. What a mistake! One of the greatest things we can do to add more enjoyment back into our lives is to refresh our female friendships again.

Girlfriends fill a role that no one else can. Men are great, but they do not make good girlfriends. They do not care about the same things women do. And most of them can't handle all of our talking! They basically let us talk but want us to tell them when they need to listen. Do they really care about the exciting new recipe you just found? Probably not, but when you tell a girlfriend, she most likely wants you to pass along the recipe. It's unfair to expect the males in your life to play the same role as your girlfriends. They aren't designed to talk for hours on the phone, to wander the shops for hours looking for just the right outfit to wear for something special, to make you laugh until tears start running down your cheeks, to share the same indecisiveness about what kind of dessert to get with your coffee until you simply cave in and end up getting one of each so you can share them.

We need to celebrate the unique role that female friendships play in our lives. Girlfriends bring out a part of us that no man can. They understand us, cry with us, laugh with us, and spend hours talking with us about our dreams and goals, our biggest fears, our disappointments, our insecurities, and our heaviest burdens. You need someone who you can simply pour your heart out to, a person to confide in. A good girlfriend makes you laugh harder and smile bigger. And the really great ones even encourage you to dream bigger and live more fully.

"A friend doesn't go on a diet because you are fat. A friend never defends a husband who gets his wife an electric skillet for her birthday. A friend will tell you she saw your old boyfriend and he's a priest." Erma Bombeck

You know those people who you just naturally click with? Those are the ones you need to treasure and celebrate. Don't let them get away. Some women have a group of close friends they've had for years, while others might have one person they feel close enough to confide in. If you have even one close friend, you are blessed. Throughout life, be on the lookout for those few precious females who you will call your closest friends. They might be a relative, a neighbor, a co-worker, a fellow church member, a stranger you met by chance, or a classmate. Friends are found in the most random of places.

I understand it's hard enough to carve out some time for yourself, let alone time for your close girlfriends. Sometimes you might even think to yourself that you don't have time for friends. But we were made to connect with people. Our soul responds when we are able to converse with a close friend. A cream and sugar break with a good friend (or friends) may be just what you need to add a little dose of fun and enjoyment to your life.

Plan some fun with one or more girlfriends. Perhaps you could do something to pamper yourself. Get manicures, pedicures, go out to eat, or grab coffee. Perhaps you want to plan a more extravagant weekend getaway together. If you have long distance friends you haven't seen recently, pick up the phone and reconnect with them. Remember, life is too short to let your friendships slide. And some of your hardest laughs come from those great friends.

Your cream and sugar breaks might be something at your own home. Invite friends over to play cards or games, host a pajama party complete with chick flicks, pizza, chips and dip, or host a good old-fashioned tea party overflowing with tea, coffee, goodies, and conversation. Another possibility is enjoying a night out on the town by treating yourselves to a movie and topping off the evening with your favorite ice cream sundaes or favorite cheesecake and coffee. Or it might be an out-of-town getaway to a Bed & Breakfast or hotel for a fun weekend. There are all kinds of girlfriend getaways catering to women that will help you relax and have fun. Rent a room, order pizza in your PJ's, eat, talk, and have fun.

Don't get so trapped by the demands of your life that you let your friendships slide. You need friends. Everyone benefits when you spend quality time with a good friend. Enjoying time with your friends makes you a happier person. You do your husband and kids a favor when you spend some quality time with a good friend. Here's the reality: if you're too busy to spend time with a good friend, you are busier than you are meant to be. Good friends make life so much sweeter.

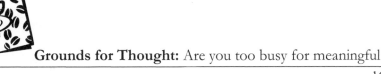 **Grounds for Thought:** Are you too busy for meaningful

friendships? When's the last time you enjoyed a fun outing with your girlfriends, mom, aunts, or sisters? Which girlfriend makes you laugh hardest?

Grounds for Action: Reflect on the friends in your life. Of those you spend time with, which ones can you totally be yourself with? Which ones make you feel so good about yourself? Pick up the phone and plan a special outing to celebrate your friendship with that person. Do something fun to enjoy a cream and sugar break together!

The Last Cup

I think we greatly underestimate the importance of fun in our lives. The more fun you have, the greater value it is on your life. Oh sure, life, just like coffee, can be experienced without the cream and sugar, but it's much richer and more enjoyable when you leave room for a little of the tastiest pleasures! There are countless fun ways to awaken and rejuvenate the part of you that gets lost in busy life. Remember to have fun, laugh, smile, and enjoy life. Pure enjoyment, practiced in even short increments each day, is great for the body and soul.

Life's cream and sugar moments are what living is all about. What do you like to do for fun? Add some of those things to your life each and every day. Scientific studies have shown that positive emotions build your emotional capacity to handle adversity and stress and to be more open and creative. If life's gotten so hectic that you don't even know what to do for fun, try new things until you find what's pleasurable for you. Schedule at least one purely enjoyable activity each week—anything that brings you happiness. Life is an adventure worth enjoying. Have fun every day!

"A merry heart makes a cheerful countenance. . ." Proverbs 15:13

GROUND RULE #10

Coffee Tastes Better When Shared ~ Love Fully

"To love and be loved is to feel the sun from both sides." David Viscott

Coffee Shared with Loved Ones is a Life Well-Lived

"You have achieved success if you have lived well, laughed often, and loved much."
Author Unknown

Of course, I drink plenty of coffee alone, but I must say that coffee simply tastes better when it's shared with others. I've realized that throughout the years, it really hasn't been the caffeine that has kept me going when I needed a lift, it's been the closeness of family and friends. That's why one of the key strategies of a joyful life is learning how to love more fully in our most important relationships. After all, relationships are more important than our accomplishments. It's not *what* you have in your life, but *whom* you have in your life that truly counts. The strength of your closest relationships will go a long way in determining your happiness in life. Just as a good cup of coffee—life, too, is best when shared.

Most of life's greatest experiences—the ones that resonate in our hearts—involve other people. Rarely do we experience these moments alone. When we do, normally our first desire is to share them with others. Think back to the most important experiences in your life—the greatest successes or the biggest challenges. How many happened to you alone? I would bet there are very few. It's the people in our lives who make good times better and difficult ones easier. When you understand that your connection to others is one of life's greatest joys, you realize that true fullness in life comes when you invest in building solid relationships.

To put it plain and simple, love is what life is all about. The love of family and friends is what fills you with life, what nurtures you and keeps you going. Yet all too often, we allow these relationships to take a much lower priority than they deserve. You've got to maintain healthy relationships with those people most precious to you—your spouse, children, family members, and closest friends. Great relationships lead to significant increase in life satisfaction. Place a high value on the people you love most. If you don't learn to fill your life with the love and friendship of others, you'll soon experience a very empty cup.

Unfortunately, because of our busy schedules, it's easy to lose sight of our most important relationships. Our busy lives can keep us disconnected from each other—even those under our own roof—and we miss out on opportunities to experience deeper connections. Relationships take time and nurturing to keep going and most of us don't have a lot of extra time. So it's easy to put others on the back burner and take them for granted as we lose ourselves in our schedules, our work, and our pursuit of personal and professional goals. The busyness of our lives doesn't allow us time to pause and appreciate the people we have around us so it's up to us to purposely make it happen.

We all need to be reminded that when we come to the end of our lives, it's not the career accomplishments, how much we got done each day, or the size of our bank accounts or homes that will matter. Our *true* worth and significance comes from the legacy we have left in the hearts and minds of those we've loved and who have loved us. When all is said and done, what will matter most are those relationships and bonds we've created with people in our lives with whom we've shared love, laughter, and memories.

"Do not let making a living prevent you from making a life." John R. Wooden

There is so much warmth to be had when we take time to nurture our most important relationships. When we make the people closest to us more of a priority, we eventually realize that the rewards are well worth the sacrifice. Our careers may be important, but our connection with loved ones is what lasts a lifetime. Our lives are made richer by the relationships we share with each other. Building solid relationships takes work and should be one of your top priorities if you want to live life to the fullest. Here are some ways to bring more joy to the relationships you hold most dear.

Grounds for Thought: Are you spending enough quality time with the people who matter most? Are there relationships you've been taking for granted? How do you show love to those around you? Do you need to start loving more fully?

JAVA JOLT #1:
Pour Time into Your Most Important Relationships

"Time is like oxygen—there's a minimum amount that's necessary for survival. And it takes quantity as well as quality to develop warm and caring relationships."
Armand Nicholi

Solid relationships don't just happen on their own. Good relationships require a lot of effort. You have to work at them. Most of us have enough on our plates to take up every bit of our time if we let it. We have careers, interests, hobbies, household responsibilities, and volunteer activities that can be very time consuming. If we want to maintain strong relationships, we must set some boundaries on our time so that we are pouring enough into our most important relationships.

Sometimes a person just needs to know you think they're worth more than anything else in this world. And you do that with the gift of time. Time shows a person they are important to you. Even if you do nothing more than simply sit and listen to them, you are still expressing love. When we give someone our undivided attention, we show them how much we care. I believe we can learn so much for this short story.

Second Cup Story:
I once read a story about an old man in his attic sorting through old books and photos, getting lost in a flood of memories. He came across an old, dusty childhood journal of his grown son, Jimmy. Opening the yellowed pages, he smiled as he read over the thoughts and reflections from his son's childhood days.

While reading this journal, he was reminded that he, too, had kept a journal of his activities through the years. He found his own journal, and placed them beside each other. The man's eyes fell upon an inscription that stood out: *Wasted the whole day fishing with Jimmy. Didn't catch a thing.*

He took his son's journal and found his entry for the same day. In large writing across the page, Jimmy's entry read: *Went fishing with Dad. Best day of my life.*

People value our time and attention more than anything else. We need to treat our family and friends like they are treasures by carving out special time for each of them—not simply the leftover time we have when we've gotten everything else done—but focused, scheduled time just for them. We need to mark it on the calendar, and make it a top priority because if we don't set these boundaries, our friends and family may end up always getting leftovers.

Without realizing it, too often we neglect those we love the most. Many people spend their good, quality time and energy at work, and they leave very little energy for the most valuable relationships in their lives. If we died tomorrow, those we work for could easily replace us in a matter of days. But the loved ones we leave behind will feel the loss for the rest of their lives. Have you been pouring yourself more into work than into your family and friendships? If so, you may want to rethink your priorities. Nobody on their deathbed ever regrets not spending more time at the office, but many regret not focusing more time with their loved ones. No deadlines, projects, or hobbies is nearly as important as the people in your life. When we get wrapped up in our busy lives, the first people to usually pay the price are those closest to us—our spouse, family, children, and friends. If responsibilities get in the way, we find ourselves making excuses to those we love in hopes they'll understand. Make it a point to recognize when you are treating your loved ones this way.

"Your job won't take care of you when you're sick. Your friends will. Stay in touch with them." Unknown

It's easy for work to take up a great portion of our lives, but it's also easy to find ourselves at home but still not spending time with our loved ones either. We miss out on so many opportunities to experience deeper connections even with those under our own roof. Too often our cell phones, computers, or the television get more attention than our loved ones. How many of you spend more time on the computer than with your spouse or children? If this sounds familiar in your household, then resolve to switch off your gadgets more often during private moments so you can nourish personal connections with complete focus. Making uninterrupted time for someone tells them that they are important to us. We are all guilty at times of neglecting important relationships. Recognize if this is happening at your home and make a commitment to give your loved ones more undivided attention.

It is so easy to take our closest loved ones for granted because we think they should 'just know' we love them. We aren't usually proactive about getting together with loved ones who don't live with us because we figure we'll just see them at the next birthday party or holiday gathering. But in doing this we miss out on much of the precious one-on-one time that's so important. Getting together with loved ones at a time when it's not required or assumed is one of the most special gifts you can give a person. Think of it this way—women love getting flowers delivered on Valentine's Day, but it's even more special when it happens during a random time throughout the year when it's not expected on a special holiday. This is similar to our time. Getting together with a loved one to celebrate a birthday, anniversary, or holiday is wonderful, but those are the times we expect to spend time. Imagine the feeling of knowing someone made time for you outside of the expected.

"Someone has written, 'Love is a verb.' It requires doing - not just saying and thinking. The test is in what one does, how one acts, for love is conveyed in word and deed." David B. Haight

Your most important relationships should come first as you plan how to spend your time. I block out time for short outings with my parents on a regular basis, taking my dad out for supper or meeting my mom for coffee. I also schedule time with my close friends to get together over lunch or coffee or sometimes to simply catch up over the phone. Carve out time to spend with your loved ones and be protective of that time. Make your family and your friendships a priority. Today you have a choice. Tomorrow you might not. Your time is priceless so share it with those you love most.

How can you find more ways to spend quality time with those who matter most to you? You could cook a sit down dinner for your family, go on a date with your spouse, invite your children on a date for ice cream cones, or schedule afternoon coffee with a friend or relative. Come up with your own list of ways to spend time with your friends and family. Getting together to spend time with one another tells the other person 'I am making time for you because you are important to me.' Getting an invitation to spend any quality time together is a special occasion.

Good relationships require an investment of time. The more love we give others, the more love we will receive. You can't have good relationships when you don't take the time to invest and put forth the effort. Decide which of your relationships are vital and pour adequate time into them. Give others the gift of your love and attention. There is simply no substitute for time. When you share time with those you love, beautiful memories will fill your life. Relationships, just like coffee, warm us up, give us enjoyment and comfort, and make life worth living. Make time. Do it now. We have no idea what is going to happen a week from now or even an hour from now. You never know how much time you will have left with the people you love. They can go at anytime—as can you. Will you look back and say, *"I wish I had made time"* or *"I'm glad I made time?"*

Grounds for Thought: How much time outside of birthdays and special occasions do you spend with those you love? In what ways have you put schedules, gadgets, or events ahead of people on your list of priorities? What percentage of time do you give to your relationships and is that 'prime time' or 'leftovers?' Are there relationships that you've been taking for granted that need your time and attention? If you didn't get another day on this earth, would your closest family and friends know how much they meant to you?

Grounds for Action: Make a list of the people you love most. How can you start expressing more love to them by making time for them? Pick up the phone and schedule lunch, dinner, coffee, a walk in the park, or some getaway time together. Or perhaps it's allowing more time for regular catch-up conversations over the phone. Get out your calendar and schedule a few hours over the coming month to spend time with your closest family and friends. Give the gift of your time to strengthen a relationship with someone you love. Taking this time sends the message, 'You are important to me.'

Extra Jolt Challenge: Leave love notes for your closest loved ones, family, and friends. Imagine you know you will not have another opportunity to see them again. What would be the lasting thoughts, words, and reflections you want to leave with them? Write them a short note to tell them how much you love them. Once you've done that, take each of them out for coffee and hand them your note. If you can't do that, then send it. Without any doubt, make sure your family and friends know you love them.

JAVA JOLT #2:
Let Unconditional Love Overflow

"Love me when I least deserve it because that's when I really need it." Swedish Proverb

Loving those closest to us isn't always going to be easy. It usually requires some sacrifice on our part. Most of the people closest to us—parents, siblings, spouses, friends, co-workers, and children—are going to let us down or hurt our feelings at some point. And that's why I think unconditional love is one of the greatest of our abilities. Loving fully requires giving ourselves a daily dose of patience, tolerance, and forgiveness. Loving unconditionally means being committed to relationships during good times and bad times. It's having the courage to accept each other as we are.

Loving unconditionally takes a considerable amount of effort and willpower. Without a doubt, people are going to disappoint us and we will disappoint them sometimes. We may have to make sacrifices, overlook something, or compromise for the good of the relationship. Perhaps another shopper cuts in front of you in the grocery store line, or a co-worker takes credit for your idea, a relative talks about you behind your back, a parent wasn't there for you, a child doesn't listen, a spouse purchases something without consulting you, or a friend lets you down by her actions. Unconditional love means that you are willing to forgive those who break your heart and show understanding by being less quick to anger when others make mistakes. It also means you stop replaying the hurtful experience again and again in your mind for weeks, months, or years. Forgive and move on. Give others the right to make some mistakes.

Every person has faults. We can't expect those around us to be perfect. Don't put unrealistic expectations on people. It's not fair to them or us. Quit demanding perfection from your spouse, kids, parents, and friends and begin accepting them as human.

Maybe you are a neat and tidy person, and your husband is known to leave his shoes and pants lying around on the bedroom floor. You've told him a thousand times to pick up his clothes, and you walk in the room, and sure enough, things are left thrown on the floor. Instead of storming into the living room and saying, *"When are you ever going to learn to put your stuff away? I'm sick and tired of cleaning up after you!"* This will only cause more strife and more division. Why don't you be the peacemaker and quietly put away his clothes and go about your way so you can enjoy your evening. Loving unconditionally means that we need to quit making a big deal out of relatively minor issues. Instead of harping on our loved ones, we need to learn to make allowances for their weaknesses.

*"My husband and I got married for better or for worse. He couldn't do any better; I couldn't do any worse."*Unknown

Do your best to create an atmosphere of peace in your home and your relationships. Certainly at times we're going to get angry or frustrated. But we don't have to say hurtful things that are going to damage our relationships. Take a step back and bite your tongue. Griping, snipping, and a critical attitude will only make things worse. If you are going to have loving relationships, you must learn to overlook some things once in awhile. We have to make adjustments in order to keep the peace. In other words, you have to pick your battles wisely. When you do your part to keep strife out of your relationships, you are loving unconditionally. And when you love unconditionally, your relationships will improve. Be willing to adapt. It's not worth losing your joy over things that don't really matter.

So often we wait for the other person to change. If you wait for someone else to change before loving them unconditionally, then you might be waiting around a whole lifetime. Relationships change when you change. Unconditional love starts with *you.* You need to make the first move. You need to be the one to keep the peace. You need to hold yourself responsible for loving more unconditionally. Of course, there are times we need to confront issues head on. But there are also more times we can choose to avoid strife by giving up our need to be right. No matter how difficult it may be, you may have to swallow your pride more often and be the bigger person so you can avoid unnecessary conflict. You may know you are right and they are wrong, but that doesn't matter.

When you decide to keep the peace, you will be blessed with stronger relationships. You will notice they get better and better.

"Love bears all things, believes all things, hopes all things, endures all things; love never ends." 1 Corinthians 13:7-8

Unconditional love requires a double dose of patience. It's being slow to anger and choosing to control your emotions rather than having them control you. It means looking past negative actions and faults and seeing that person for who he or she is down deep and encouraging them to be the best they can be. Patience does not come naturally to any of us. But wise women realize it's an essential ingredient for their relationships and a great way to express unconditional love. Be patient and sensitive to the needs of those you love. It requires a load of self-sacrifice as you offer to help your aging parents even when you need help yourself, or as you comfort your child who just broke one of your grandmother's antique dishes, or as you try to encourage and support a loved one who's spoken harshly to you in the past or to love a spouse who has difficultly showing love back.

Loving unconditionally also means giving those you love the space to grow and to make mistakes. Times will not always be easy and things will go wrong once in awhile. We can learn a great lesson on how to handle times like these from this story.

**Second Cup Story:**

A woman received a brand new car from her husband for a wedding gift. One day while driving from the store, she took the corner too quickly and sideswiped another car. The lady pulled over to the side of the road, and the driver of the other car, an older gentleman, got out of his car to examine his severely damaged front bumper. He then walked over to where she was still sitting and crying in her car. *"Are you ok, young lady?"* he asked kindly.

"I'm fine," she sobbed. *"But I just got married and my husband gave me this car as a wedding present. He's going to be so upset, and I don't know what I'm going to do!"*

The older man tried to console her, saying, *"I'm sure it's going to be ok.*

Your husband will understand." They talked for a few minutes and then the man asked that they just trade insurance information and both be on their way. *"But I don't even know if I have an insurance card,"* she said through her tears.

"Well, it's usually in the glove compartment," he suggested, *"so why don't you look in there?"* She opened the glove compartment to search for the registration and insurance information. She found an envelope that contained both of them and attached to this envelope was a note, written by her husband that read, *Honey, just in case you ever have an accident, just remember: I love you—not the car.*

That's the same kind of understanding we need to have with those around us. Rather than flaunting other people's failures, wrong actions, and mistakes, learn to accept some of those mistakes in the people who are closest to you. Don't be controlling or demanding of those you love because if you are, you are not striving to love without conditions. Love people with your whole heart and be understanding, caring and patient.

Another key aspect to loving unconditionally is forgiving those who have hurt you by getting rid of any old pain, anger and grudges you've been carrying with you day after day. You can't keep score of the way others have wronged you and expect to make your relationships right. If there is someone who's hurt you or you haven't spoken to in years, don't wait until you can't make amends. Do it today. Let bygones be bygones. Life is too short to be critical and stubborn. Keep the peace even if you weren't in the wrong. Remember, it's not always about being right; it's about loving unconditionally. You can win every argument, but if it brings division and tears you apart, you didn't win at all. In the quest to prove a point, pride chips away at love. Don't focus on being right; focus on being happy. If someone has hurt you and you need to address it and get it out, then do it now. Forgive those who have hurt you and move on. Resolving past hurts makes room for much more love to enter your heart.

"Forgiveness does not equal forgetting. It is about healing the memory of the harm, not erasing it." Ken Hart

Are you someone who keeps a mental list of everything someone's done wrong to you over your life? Keeping score of when your boss was rude, a parent said something hurtful, your friend forgot to send a birthday card, or your husband missed the kids' ballgame? Unconditional love doesn't keep record of wrongs done. Stop replaying everything that people have done wrong to you. As long as you bring up pain from the past, you are going to have pain in the present. Be a peacekeeper, not a record keeper. You will see your relationships move to a whole new level if you just get rid of the record book.

Loving unconditionally also requires purposely trying to see the good in another when you're tempted to judge them. When you truly love unconditionally, you do not set limits on the amount of love you will give. Instead, you love a person no matter what they do, say, believe, or look like. And you love them without stipulations or expecting love or rewards in return. Sometimes we overlook those who are not just like us or those who are just plain difficult to love. But everyone needs to know they are valued and loved. In fact, you might be the only person who acknowledges them all day. Work hard to see people without their faults, limitations, disabilities, or deformities and see them as someone who needs and deserves your unconditional love.

To get to a place of total acceptance and love, you need to pour cupfuls of patience, understanding, tolerance, and forgiveness onto those around you—those who disappoint you, challenge your every nerve, hurt you, or disappoint you. Never give up on your loved ones. Love people even when they are most difficult to love, and forgive them with an open heart when they have hurt you. When you do this, you are pouring unconditional love onto others.

"Love is patient, love is kind, love does not insist on its own way. Love bears all things, believes all things, hopes all things, endures all things. Love never fails."
1 Corinthians 13: 4-8

Grounds for Thought: Can your spouse and/or kids count on having a patient wife and mother? How are you allowing frustrations to overshadow the positive qualities of your loved ones? How can you be a more loving wife, mother, daughter, sister, and friend? Is there someone you have to learn to be more understanding with (parent, child, spouse, relative, or co-worker)? Who do you have trouble accepting? Are you harboring any resentment or grudges? Have you ever treated someone unfairly because they didn't look or act like you do?

Grounds for Action: Make a list of those who test your patience. Now, begin to look for the positives in these people. When you begin to look for the positives instead of focusing on their negatives, it allows you to enjoy this person much more each day. And people naturally respond by being much nicer to you. Make a vow to say nothing negative to those people on your list today. Instead, do one expected gesture of kindness for them.

Next, forgive someone who's hurt you. Get rid of any old hurts and disappointments that are weighing on you. Take steps toward improving a relationship in your life.

JAVA JOLT #3:
Create Warm Traditions

"Love doesn't make the world go round. Love is what makes the ride worthwhile."
Franklin P. Jones

Stop for a moment and remember some of your fondest moments. Most of life's greatest memories involve people you care deeply for. One of my most cherished memories from my childhood is the precious time I spent with my Grandma. She was an excellent baker, and I was always so eager to learn from her. I remember how excited I'd get when she would take warm sugar cookies out of the oven, and I'd watch Grandma pour two cups of coffee for our coffee breaks together—she'd drink her coffee, and I'd dunk my cookies into my coffee. My Grandma was so special. Her eagerness to spend time with me, to teach me how to bake, and to share our 'coffee breaks' together made me feel special and loved.

Creating memories like this that we can cherish for years to come is one of the most precious gifts in life. The most meaningful moments are those that we share with the people we love the most. Think of it this way: if I asked you to make a list of all the birthday or Christmas gifts you've received over the past five years, how many could you list? Now, make a list of the special times you've had with loved ones during those same years. I'd be willing to bet you were able to remember more of the special times than the presents you received, right? Cherished memories are the greatest gifts we receive and why it's so important to intentionally create warm traditions with those closest to you. Treasured memories are created by sharing and embracing the moments of life with people we love. Isn't it wonderful to know we have the opportunity to design these kinds of experiences? We don't have to wait for them to come to us.

Creating loving, memorable traditions provides an opportunity to strengthen the bonds of love in our relationships by helping us grow our relationships, discover new things together, laugh together, and to have lots of fun. Traditions are a way to show others how much you love and care about them. And the memories these times create turn them into something lasting. Traditions give you a shared history and identity with those you enjoy them with. Celebrate the warmth and intimacy of your relationships by doing fun things together and establishing special traditions to share with those you love most.

My mom and aunts hold a tradition of getting together annually for some type of Sister's Weekend. This is time simply to be together and reconnect. Sister's Weekend involves lots of fun, lots of talking, lots of eating and lots of laughter. They typically don't care where they go as long as they are together. Traditions like this help them renew their bonds of sisterhood when busy lives make it difficult.

Doing things together is what makes great memories. Create as many positive experiences as you can with those you love. Start thinking of ways you can create traditions with your closest loved ones. You could meet for monthly dinner dates, get together for monthly Inspirational Coffee Club meetings, bake Christmas cookies together annually, take an annual getaway with friends or sisters, go on an annual Bed & Breakfast weekend with your spouse, write daily notes on your child's lunchbox napkin, plant a family garden, make the last Friday night of every month a pizza and games/movies night, hold monthly theme suppers with friends, schedule a weekly TV night with your spouse or girlfriends to watch your favorite show, or plan weekly phone calls to a long distant sibling, parent, or friend. The greatest bonds between people come as the result of their experiences together. Find ways to create moments with your family and friends that infuse lasting love into your experiences. Creating warm traditions is a great way to strengthen your relationships.

Grounds for Thought: Are you creating meaningful family moments? Do you have special traditions you are creating with your loved ones? What past memories still make you smile? What's the most special memory you have from your childhood?

Grounds for Action: Start creating more traditions with your family and friends. Make a list of some activities you could do to spend more time and create more memories together. Fun and meaningful traditions are numerous and their impact can be felt for years. Making lasting memories will strengthen those relationships you cherish most.

JAVA JOLT #4:
Always Make Time for Coffee With Mom

"Mothers are those wonderful people who can get up in the morning before the smell of coffee." Author Unknown

As I grow older, what I cherish most are my relationships but specifically my relationship with my mom. It's one of the relationships I value most highly in my life. I've been very fortunate to be able to develop a close bond with her. We've created so many wonderful memories together.

For years, we've shared a weekly tradition of meeting for morning coffee. This time with my mom is my favorite time of the week. These regular coffee gatherings are a way I get to celebrate my treasured relationship with her. As often as we can, we meet for a cup of coffee— sometimes short, sometimes longer. We love visiting different coffee houses each time, until we settle on a couple favorites (typically the ones with the best caramel rolls!) These little coffee breaks, though they might be simple, are a symbol of our love.

When I call my mom and say, *"Hey, want to grab coffee this morning?"* she knows what I really mean—that I want to spend time with her. I want to connect with her because she matters to me. 'Meeting for coffee' really means so much more than just the beverage. Each coffee break represents time together and every cup of coffee shared is a token of my love for her. And I want to take every chance I can to show her that I love her.

The bond between a mother and daughter is one of the most important relationships in life. If you are fortunate to still have your mother or a daughter of your own, start developing special mother-daughter traditions you can treasure for a lifetime. Personally, I recommend taking coffee breaks together and enjoying drinks and treats over conversation. But it might also be a yearly Bed & Breakfast outing, a daily phone call, a monthly visit, going to Sunday church together, or having dinner together every Saturday.

"God could not be everywhere, so he created Mothers." Jewish Proverb

Recently, I was talking to a friend about how important my mom is to me. I was moved by an experience she shared with me. That same day she had taken her 93-year old mom to the beauty shop to get her hair done and had parked in front of the door to help her mom from the car. An impatient lady in a car behind her opened up her car door and said, *"Ma'am, I'm trying to leave here. Can you please move your car?"* My friend said to that driver, *"Just one minute please. I'm unloading my mom and her walker."* The other driver quickly calmed down and said, *"That's fine. I wish I had a mother to unload."*

If you are fortunate to still have your mother (or someone who's been like a mother to you), spend time with her. Let her know you care. Don't get too busy with the 'small stuff' in life. We can learn much from this illustration.

Second Cup Story:

When things in your life seem almost too much to handle, when 24-hours in a day are not enough, remember this story about a mayonnaise jar and two cups of coffee...

A professor stood before his philosophy class and had some items in front of him. When the class began, wordlessly, he picked up a very large and empty mayonnaise jar and proceeded to fill it with golf balls. He then asked the students if the jar was full. They agreed that it was.

So the professor then picked up a box of pebbles and poured them into the jar. He shook the jar lightly. The pebbles rolled into the open areas between the golf balls. He then asked the students again if the jar was full. They agreed it was.

The professor next picked up a box of sand and poured it into the jar. Of course, the sand filled up everything else. He asked once more if the jar was full. The students responded with a unanimous, *"yes."*

The professor then produced two cups of coffee from under the table and poured the entire contents into the jar, effectively filling the empty space between the sand. The students laughed. *"Now,"* said the professor, as the laughter subsided, *"I want you to recognize that this jar represents your life. The golf balls are the important things- God, your family, your children, your health, your friends, and your favorite passions-things that if everything else was lost and only they remained, your life would still be full. The pebbles are the other things that matter like your job, your house, and your car. The sand is everything else-the small stuff."*

"If you put the sand into the jar first," he continued, *"there is no room for the pebbles or the golf balls. The same goes for life. If you spend all your time and energy on the small stuff, you will never have room for the things that are important."*

So, pay attention to the things that are most important. Take care of your health, your faith, and spend time with those you love. There's always time to clean the house—it's a never-ending job anyway. Take care of the golf balls first, the things that really matter. Set your priorities. The rest is just sand.

Wondering what the coffee represents? No matter how full your life may seem, there's always room for a couple cups of coffee with a loved one.

There are so many little ways to show your mom you love her without even saying it. Be sure to treat your mom like your favorite coffee break companion. My advice-always make time for coffee with mom.

"I know of no more permanent imprint on a life than the one made by mothers."
Charles Swindoll

Grounds for Thought: How do you say 'I love you' to your mom without even saying it? Are you spending enough time with her? If she died today, would you have any doubts that she didn't know how much she was loved?

Grounds for Action: If you are fortunate to still have your mom (or a person who's been like a mother to you), take her on a coffee outing. Just the two of you. Enjoy coffee and desserts and treasure each other's company. If your mom is miles away, schedule your coffee break over the phone. Each grab your favorite mugs and enjoy a cup of coffee or tea while visiting with each other on the other end. Celebrate your mom.

The Last Cup

Being connected to others is one of life's great joys. Most of life's best moments—the ones that stay in our hearts and minds—involve other people. Yet the sad truth is that we tend to take those closest to us the most for granted. Make sure those who have nurtured you, mothered you, befriended you, and loved you unconditionally know how much they mean to you. And make sure you say all the things you want to say before it's too late. Get your priorities straight.

Seek opportunities to put more love into the world. Strive to fill those around you with more compassion and kindness. In turn, it makes you more lovable. There are infinite ways to pour more love to those around you—spend more quality time, be more patient, forgiving, and tolerant. Above all, cherish the time you have with those closest to you, and let each person know how special they are to you. Make every relationship count; there is no better time to show your love than today.

The way you approach your relationships has a profound impact on how you live. If you're willing to put quality time and energy into them, your closest family and friends become a source of fulfillment and strength. My greatest memories are filled with the people who mean the most to me. Bring joy to the relationships you hold most dear because nothing else in life is as fulfilling as the relationships we cultivate. Our lives are made richer by the relationships we share with each other. Let love overflow to those around you. Start loving more fully today because without a doubt, coffee tastes better when shared.

"The best and most beautiful things in life cannot be seen, not touched, but are felt in the heart." Helen Keller

GROUND RULE #11

A Cracked Cup is a Treasure ~
Triumph Over Trials

"We cannot tell what may happen to us in the strange medley of life, but we can decide what happens in us—how we take it, what we do with it—and that is what really counts in the end. How we take the raw stuff of life and make a thing of worth and beauty—that is the test of living." Joseph Fort Newton

Life's "Cracks" Make You a Treasure

"Character cannot be developed in ease and quiet. Only through experience of trial and suffering can the soul be strengthened, ambition inspired, and success achieved." Helen Keller

We all have experiences that we wish we didn't have to go through—a loss of a loved one, financial difficulties, failed relationships, illnesses, work conflicts, family issues, an unexpected move, abuse, injury, infertility, loss of a dream—just to name a few. I'm confident your life has not always been easy. There are certain inevitable events that happen to each of us. The world is full of what I call "cracks" in our cups—troubles that come into our life regardless if we want them or not and leave us feeling shattered, powerless, and weakened. These "cracks" attempt to damage or break us, and sometimes they may get pretty darn close. Even though our lives may be fragile, we become so much more valuable from every adversity we triumph through.

One of my favorite coffee mugs (one I received from my mom years ago) has multiple miniature cracks, but it's still useable, and it's still my favorite. In fact, I treat it much more delicately because it means so much to me. Just as a well-used cup has chips in the rim, a life well-lived has chips in the soul. Life's "cracks" do not make you worthless and unusable. They make you more precious. Your cup represents one beautiful, fragile, irreplaceable thing—your own life. Every mistake you've made, every obstacle you've overcome, and every challenge you've endured is part of the woman you are today. These make you a real treasure.

Though the pain you experience from your "cracks" may dull over time, the "cracks" in your cup will never disappear. They are part of who you are. In fact, you'll probably gain more and more of them over the years. They will always be there—reminding us of loved ones we've lost, illnesses suffered, opportunities gone, relationships ended, financial struggles—all those times that have attempted to break us. But you are *not* broken. Remember, these "cracks" are a measure of a life well-lived. And you are more valuable because of them. Never, ever forget that a cracked cup is a treasure. If you don't believe me, let this story be a reminder.

 **Second Cup Story:**

An elderly Chinese woman had two large pots, each hung on the ends of a pole which she carried across her neck. One of the pots had a crack in it while the other pot was perfect and always delivered a full portion of water. At the end of the long walks from the stream to the house, the cracked pot arrived only half full.

For a full two years this went on daily, with the woman bringing home only one and a half pots of water. Of course, the perfect pot was proud of its accomplishments. But the poor cracked pot was ashamed of its own imperfection, and miserable that it could only do half of what it had been made to do.

After two years of what it perceived to be a bitter failure, it spoke to the woman one day by the stream. *"I am ashamed of myself because this crack in my side causes water to leak out all the way back to your house."*

The old woman smiled, *"Did you notice that there are flowers on your side of the path, but not on the other pot's side? That's because I have always known about your flaw, so I planted flower seeds on your side of the path, and every day while we walk back, you water them. For two years I have been able to pick these beautiful flowers to decorate the table. Without you being just the way you are, there would not be this beauty to grace the house."*

Each of us has our own unique 'flaws' (which are not defects). You have to take each "crack" as it comes and look for the value in it. Life is going to hand each one of us painful experiences. The richer our lives, the more likely we are to experience the pain of "cracks" in our cups. If we have lots of cherished friends and loved ones, we will have to deal with more goodbyes. In addition, the more risks we take and dreams we follow, the greater likelihood we are going to experience some type of disappointment or failure. Though we can't predict or prevent most of life's challenges, we can change how we handle them and what we do with them. Those who live life to the fullest not only survive challenges but become more valuable because of them. They don't only endure trials; they triumph over them becoming a more wise, loving, and wonderful woman with each victory. Let me give you a few strategies for turning your cracked cup into a treasure.

Grounds for Thought: Are you facing any personal battles that seem daunting right now? Have you experienced painful situations and challenges in the past that you wish you would not have had to go through? How have those affected your life today?

JAVA JOLT #1:
Cracks are Common but Brokenness is Optional

"Strength does not come from winning. Your struggles develop your strengths. When you go through hardships and decide not to surrender, that is strength." Arnold Schwarzenegger

You've heard the phrase, *What doesn't break you will only make you stronger.* Well, it's true. (In which case most of us could be body builders by now!) Refusing to be broken by adversity is one of the most powerful decisions you can ever make in your life. None of us can avoid trials, but we can make sure we don't let our spirit die with them. Life's troubles can only break you if you let them. You have a choice if you'll allow your circumstances to break you or use them to make you stronger. Cracks are common, but brokenness is optional. When you are faced with a major setback, *you* have to decide whether your story will be one of perseverance and triumph or one of defeat and failure.

Sometimes you are going to encounter what seems like overwhelming odds in life. Overcoming life's challenges is not easy. Cracks attempt to leave you broken physically, emotionally, and mentally. You can spend months or years wedged in the hollows of pain, sadness, and despair. Many people are undone by crisis, keeping themselves stuck in a hole of hopelessness, anger, guilt, fear, and depression. If you believe that a situation in your life is hopeless, you sit back and let yourself be destroyed. When this happens, you often become bitter, negative, hardened, and subsequently, broken. But if you stay broken, your life will never get better.

If you don't want to remain broken, you must get up each day, tell yourself your situation is not hopeless, and try to create meaning and purpose from what life is handing you. You have to refuse to give up. Even when there seems to be no way, there's always a way. You have to purposely decide to rise out of the cracks, filling the hollows with perseverance, faith, and courage. Otherwise, your cracks will attempt to distract you from what is still left in life. Get control over your sadness, frustration, and anger because they are what will leave you broken. Replace them with renewed hope and possibilities and you'll find strength you never knew you had.

"Promise me you'll always remember: You're braver than you believe and stronger than you seem and smarter than you think." Christopher Robin to Pooh

Sure, a part of you feels broken but so much more of you is still strong and still whole. Instead of dwelling on the pain of that crack, start focusing on the parts of your life that are still whole. Be glad in what you still have. You may have lost a cherished loved one too soon, but be grateful you have other loved ones and friends around you. Perhaps you've lost your job, but you still have a great support system to carry you through. Find a way out of your cracks and into what's left of your life. Trust life enough to give it another chance after your difficulties.

Those who turn their cracks into treasures not only refuse to be broken, but they also use every challenge as an opportunity to grow stronger—emotionally, spiritually, and physically. Many people lift themselves out of the despair and pain, acquiring a whole new kind of inner strength. After all, we grow far more in the hard times than in the times when everything is going well. These cracks can strengthen us for the things that come in the future and leave us equipped to handle any adversity that comes in life. Consider the story of the butterfly.

**Second Cup Story:**
The Beautiful Butterfly (Author Unknown)

A man found a cocoon of a butterfly. One day a small opening appeared. He sat and watched the butterfly for several hours as it struggled to force its body through that little hole. Then it seemed to stop making any progress. It appeared as if it had gotten as far as it could, and it could go no further. So the man decided to help the butterfly. He took a pair of scissors and snipped off the remaining bit of the cocoon. The butterfly then emerged easily. But it had a swollen body and small, shriveled wings.

The man continued to watch the butterfly because he expected that, at any moment, the wings would enlarge and expand to be able to support the body, which would contract in time. Neither happened! In fact, the butterfly spent the rest of its life crawling around with a swollen body and shriveled wings. It never was able to fly.

What the man, in his kindness and haste, did not understand was that the restricting cocoon and the struggle required for the butterfly to get through the tiny opening were God's way of forcing fluid from the body of the butterfly into its wings so that it would be ready for flight once it achieved its freedom from the cocoon.

If we went through life without any obstacles, it would cripple us. *We would not be as strong as what we could have been, and we could never fly!*

Many of our difficulties cannot be removed. But we can use those things to make us stronger, better women. It's in the tough times when we develop our character. Truthfully we don't grow near as much when everything is easy. We grow when it's most difficult. Think back to the worst experience you've gone through. Was there a time when you wondered how you'd ever get through it? But you did. You pushed through it and you are here. And didn't you learn you were stronger than you ever thought possible?

Don't allow yourself to be broken by your hardships. It's how we respond to our trials that makes the most difference. Learn to look pain and suffering straight in the eyes, and refuse to let it crumble you. When we have the right outlook, we can overcome and be victorious over any situation. It is up to us whether we live in victory or defeat. Choose not to be broken. Just because you have had moments of weaknesses, don't believe you are weak. You have more strength than you know! Stop fighting the cracks. Instead, use your struggles to make you stronger. Accept the cracks and embrace every single one of them as an opportunity to grow into a more resilient, more loving woman. In this way, although our lives may still seem fragile, it's impossible to be broken. Never, ever give up!

"Being defeated is only a temporary condition; giving up is what makes it permanent." Marilyn vos Savant

Grounds for Thought: What challenges in your life have threatened to break you, leaving you so discouraged and hopeless that you just felt like giving up? Are there any trials leaving you broken right now? To this point in your life, have you chosen to see these cracks in your cup as events that make you stronger or events that weaken you? As painful as your cracks are, what did you learn about your level of courage and personal strength? Can you remember the times you refused to give up?

Grounds for Action: Make a list of all the cracks in your life (big and small ones). Put an 'S' by those that made you a stronger woman. Put a 'B' next to those that are still keeping you broken. Don't be ashamed to cry for those experiences that are still leaving you broken. God purposely made tears to help us relieve our pain. Cry as long as you need to until you feel a sense of peace with your situation.

Look through that list of cracks and say out loud, *"I will not give up! I can handle anything that happens to me. I am growing stronger and stronger."* Repeat this every time life's challenges seem to be crushing down on you.

"Weeping may endure for a night, but joy comes in the morning." Psalm 30:5

JAVA JOLT #2:
Each Crack is Wisdom in Disguise

"The highest reward for a person's toil is not what they get for it, but what they become by it." John Ruskin

Those of you who have recently experienced cracks may be wondering if life will ever feel 'normal' again, or if the pain ever goes away. When tragedy or difficulty strikes, nothing can fix what happened.

We go on, but that crack will leave an ache in our hearts for a long time, possibly forever. We can't go back to how we were so give up trying to get back to 'normal.' You will never be the exact same woman again. Moving forward isn't about getting rid of the cracks; it's about transforming them. We have to meet these cracks with a new outlook, learning to adapt to our new self with new cracks. Though your cup won't be exactly how it was before, it can become a different, more valuable one if you choose to see those cracks as wisdom in disguise instead of flaws and limitations. Over time, you will begin to develop a new normal—one that takes into account the new changes in your life: life without a loved one, without the job you had, with a new diagnosis, and so forth.

As challenging as it may seem, there is a lesson for growth and wisdom that can be learned from every crack in our cup. Every event, no matter how disappointing, unpleasant, discouraging or difficult a situation, is a chance to learn something new about yourself. Your life experiences are what shape you into the amazing person you are meant to be. If you hadn't gone through these, you wouldn't be the same person you are today. There is great wisdom we can only attain through great struggle and setbacks.

Society is filled with stories of people who have come through tragedy to find new or different meaning in their lives. I read an interview featuring Michael J. Fox who has lost control over his own body from Parkinson's disease. He sums up the outcome of his struggle with this sentence, *"For everything this disease has taken, something with greater value has been given."*

Have any of your struggles brought you wisdom in some way? Maybe you lost a child, spouse, or sibling far too early, but did this loss bring you a renewed appreciation to those loved ones still here with you? Or perhaps you went through a devastating job loss, but did this allow you to discover undeveloped talents or unexplored opportunities? Or maybe you were stunned by the news of an unexpected pregnancy, but when you look back now, you realize it's given you a new sense of purpose for living. Or perhaps a diagnosis of an unexpected illness knocked you down, but through it all, your circle of support and love grew stronger and deeper than ever before. Perhaps you went through a difficult break-up that eventually turned out to give you an invigorated confidence in your abilities.

"Human experience would lose something if there were no limitations to overcome. The hilltop hour would not be so wonderful if there were no dark valleys to traverse."
Helen Keller

The ability to find positive meaning even during our challenging times is what seems to make such a difference. Life can be harder but deeper too. Learn to grow with the changes. Rather than focus on what was lost, unfair, or taken from you, resilient people focus on how this has made them build deeper faith and deeper sense of character. You can either look at painful life events as unfair or use them as a means to make you a wiser, more caring, insightful woman who lives every day without taking a single day for granted.

Our difficult times are filled with opportunities to become a better person by giving us a greater ability to empathize with others—to be more sensitive to those around us, to be less judgmental and more tolerant, to give us more capacity to be patient, to make us more thoughtful, loving, kind, tender and caring, to grow us spiritually, and to make us appreciate and live life more fully. As you begin to draw out the wisdom of your experiences, you can use what's happened to you to impact other people's lives as well as your own.

You can't change what has happened to you, but you can use your trials to be a blessing and inspiration for others. Perhaps the best way to heal your own sorrow is to help heal someone else's grief. Share the wisdom and insights you've received from your life experiences to provide hope and comfort to others who are facing (or will face) similar trials. I've found that I'm a much better friend and sympathizer having going through the experiences I have. Use what you've learned to help others who are facing insurmountable cracks themselves. In doing so, you turn your trials into blessings for others. Consider this true story of how a mother took her tragic life events and turned them into a means to help others.

**Second Cup Story:**
In June 1986, Lonise Bias's son Len, considered to be one of the greatest up-and-coming young basketball stars, was drafted by the Boston Celtics to play at the professional level. But two days after the draft, her

son died of a cocaine overdose, never getting the chance to pursue his NBA dreams. Four years later, Lonise tragically lost a second son, Jay, who was murdered in a drive-by-shooting at the age of 20.

From that sadness and sometimes overwhelming grief, Lonise Bias found a mission: to share a message of tragedy and hope to inspire others. Although the deaths of both her sons have been described in the press as "senseless," they were not because Lonise has refused to let them be. For the past 20 years, this brave mother has worked to give meaning to her unspeakable loss by bringing some good out of it to help others. Lonise tours the country talking about her sons' deaths. She has become an anti-drug lecturer teaching youth the devastating effects of drugs, hoping to help other parents avoid a similar tragedy. And her husband, James, has become an advocate for handgun control.

Lonise learned the lesson of turning her trials into triumphs. Even in the shadows of her sons' tragic deaths, she teaches a message of hope to those around her. We can learn so much from her story about overcoming our own personal hardships. Rather than asking, *"Why do I have to suffer?"* we should ask, *"How can my suffering help another?"* There are people out there who really need you. Others who can learn from what you have gone through. You could be the answer to someone's prayer. Seek out opportunities to share the wisdom you've gained through your difficult experiences to help others. Be a blessing to someone. It's amazing how God can use you to touch other people's lives.

"Very few burdens are heavy if everyone lifts." Unknown

Triumphing over our trials doesn't come from getting around our suffering, but from going through it. Trials can be some of the most powerful transformational experiences of our lives if we look for the lesson instead of focusing only on our sadness and frustration. Perhaps the hardest thing to remember in the midst of our pain and sadness is that every bad break can also be a valuable growth experience. Indeed, there is always wisdom in adversity, provided we meet our trials with a shift in outlook. Once you have handled those situations and find the lesson for personal growth, you never emerge the same person you were before the crack. Take time to think about your life and to harvest the lessons you've learned. Every challenge is wisdom disguised as a crack.

Grounds for Thought: Have you ever been able to use your difficulties to help someone else through theirs? Has hearing about someone else's struggles ever given you comfort during your own? What can others learn from you from watching how you handle life's challenges? Have you used your trials to make you a 'better' woman or have they made you a 'bitter' woman?

Grounds for Action: Take a life wisdom break. Review the major cracks in your life cup. Make a list of lessons you've learned about life from your most difficult life experiences. What advice can you share with others? Or perhaps it's lessons you've learned from someone else (a daughter or sibling fighting a serious illness, a friend going through a divorce). How can you use the wisdom you've learned from your challenges to make life better for someone else? Think of someone you know who could use your loving wisdom and encouragement right now to help them through their circumstance. In doing so, you will comfort and heal yourself.

It may first seem that you can't find any lessons in your difficult experiences, but if you stick with it, you will eventually see the light. At first you may need to cry, vent, be angry, and simply experience the raw emotions that go with it. But in order to move on with joy, you have to look for the growth. If you make a sincere effort to look for the good in any situation, you will eventually find it. Then your whole experience will change. This is a key part of creating real value in your life from your trials.

JAVA JOLT #3:
Faith and Prayer are Incredible Superglue

"I know God will not give me anything I can't handle; I just wish He didn't trust me so much." Mother Teresa

Life can indeed deal us some devastating blows, and at times, we might find ourselves on the brink of despair. Who hasn't wanted to shake her fist and scream, *"Why?"* This question can wrack our thoughts until the pain is almost unbearable. When our breaks make us most fragile, more than ever we need to cling to faith and prayer. They are the superglue that holds us together when we are at our weakest. Sometimes they are the only thing that can keep us together when we're on the brink of brokenness, when life doesn't make sense, and when we simply can't see beyond the pain. Without them, triumphing over trials will be much more difficult.

There is a certain strength that only God can give us. Being able to place your pains, worries, and doubts in God's hands gives you a comfort that nobody else can. One of my all-time favorite Bible verses is Philippians 4:13: *"I can do all things through Christ who strengthens me."* I repeat it many times when I feel as if I'm on the brink of breaking down. When I face challenges that seem daunting, I envision my cracked, fragile cup being held in God's steady hands as a precious treasure—cracks and all. Whenever you feel like your world is falling apart, hang in there! God's got your cup and stands beside you in your deepest pain. He never leaves you even when you feel like you may shatter at any moment. If you put yourself in God's hands, you simply cannot be broken.

"Blessed are those who mourn, for they will be comforted." Matthew 5:4

Faith and prayer can keep us going even when nothing's going well. They give us hope that the future we place in God's hands will be better than the present we hold in ours—that there will be a better tomorrow, and there's light at the end of the tunnel. In our trials, we often face pain that we feel no one else sees or understands. However, God sees our needs and understands the burdens that we bear. If we let Him, He will bear the load with us. He will enable us to get through anything if we just trust in Him. Don't ever feel your situation is hopeless.

Understand that your faith will not deliver you out of every problem. God does not promise us that we will never feel pain or sorrow, but He has promised to be present with us through it. Let your faith be the superglue to carry you through your trials. Most of us are going to go through times that attempt to test our faith by causing us to question *'why?'* One of the most important aspects of faith is trusting God even when you don't understand. You need to accept that you will not have answers for *'why?'* The simple truth is that we may never know why bad things happen to us, but God lets us know how to walk through them with faith. Make a decision to turn your most difficult situations over to God in prayer, and then move to a place of faith, optimism, and hope. Triumphing over trials means learning to trust God when the situation is out of your hands.

You may be fighting some serious battles, but the good news is that you don't have to stop living your life. When a person has a deep faith, it helps them rebound from difficult events more easily. You may have lost your job, a child or parent might be sick, you may be facing huge financial struggles, or dealing with a difficult divorce. Keep pressing forward, trusting God. Remind yourself that even though you don't know what you might have to go through next, rest assured that your cup rests strong in His hands.

If you're in a tough place right now, spend some time reaching out to God. Ask Him for renewed hope and strength when your circumstances look bleak or even impossible. As difficult as it is to believe, this I know is true: God has a plan for each of us. God knows the cracks we've experienced. His plans for us are good, although they may look different than we expected. He can use every situation to strengthen our faith and make us more valuable.

Many times in our lives we are dropped, cracked, and chipped by the decisions we make and the circumstances that come our way. Our struggles can make us feel as though we are worthless. But no matter what has happened or what will happen, you will never lose your value in God's eyes. Cracks and all, you are still *priceless* to Him. He can take your struggles and use them to help you become the woman you are meant to be. Through Him, we can triumph over our trials.

Happiness Keeps You Sweet,
Trials Keep You Strong,
Sorrows Keep You Human,
Failures Keep You Humble,
Success Keeps You Glowing,
But Only God Keeps You Going.
Author Unknown

Grounds for Thought: Do you lean on God for support during your trials? How has your faith helped you conquer a difficult situation? Have you experienced events that have tested your faith or made you want to question God? What difficulties do you need to pass over to God in prayer? How has going through tough times helped you come to better know God?

Grounds for Action: Say a prayer. Ask God to place your cup and the cups of your loved ones in His loving hands. When your challenges seem insurmountable, repeat this verse to give you hope and strength: *"I can do all things through Christ who strengthens me."* (Philippians 4:13) May you always feel cradled in the hand of God like the cherished woman you are.

The Last Cup

There will likely be much pain and suffering we endure throughout our lifetime. We cannot eliminate all our sorrows, but we don't have to allow them to ruin our joy. When you look back over your life, you'll see that those times of pain and suffering provided the greatest growth. They have made you the strong, wonderful woman you are today. Learning to triumph over trials means finding a way to manage your cracks rather than letting them crumble away your enjoyment of life.

The way in which we accept and choose to see these experiences and our suffering is what either adds deeper meaning to our lives or what makes us more fragile and weak. Instead of seeing every difficult or challenging event as a negative, see it as an opportunity to learn important insight about yourself and how you want to live your life. When you find personal meaning and growth from each crack in your life, you open your heart and soul to fully letting yourself become more valuable. Your cracked cup is what makes you unique.

You may be going through tough times, but remember, you are stronger than you ever realized. Some things you may never understand—why you got sick, why your loved one died, why you weren't able to have children, why you lost your job, why your marriage broke up, why that hereditary illness affects your family, or why you were abused. If you are always trying to figure it out, it will only bring frustration, confusion, and sadness. It may not be easy, but you've got to trust that you can use every situation that's come into your life to make you the woman you are meant to become.

Your cracks will always be there—they don't go away—but you are not broken and your future is not hopeless. When you look at the impact that difficult past experiences have had on your life, I hope you see each crack as a representation of a life well-lived; one full of love, sacrifice, opportunity, perseverance, and triumph. A cracked cup is a treasure. Therefore, you are a masterpiece.

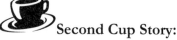**Second Cup Story:**
Are you a carrot, an egg, or a coffee bean? (Author Unknown)

A young woman was visiting with her mother, telling her all about her life, and how things were so hard for her. She did not know how she was going to make it and wanted to give up. She was tired of fighting and struggling. It seemed as one problem was solved, a new one arose.

Her mother took her to the kitchen. She filled three pots with water. In the first pot, she placed carrots; in the second, she placed eggs, and in the last, she placed ground coffee beans. She let them sit and boil without saying a word. In about twenty minutes, she turned off the burners. She fished the carrots out and placed them in a bowl. She pulled the eggs out and placed them in a bowl. Then she ladled the coffee out and placed it in a bowl. Turning to her daughter, she asked, *"Tell me, what do you see?"*

"Carrots, eggs, and coffee," she replied. She brought her closer and asked her to feel the carrots. She did and noted they were soft. She then asked her to take the egg and break it. After pulling off the shell, she observed the hard-boiled egg. Finally, she asked her to smell and sip the coffee. The daughter smiled as she smelled and tasted its rich aroma. The daughter then asked, *"What's the point, mother?"*

Her mother explained that each of these objects had faced the same adversity—boiling water—but each reacted differently. The carrot went in strong, hard, and unrelenting. However, after being subjected to the boiling water, it softened and became weak. The egg had been fragile. Its thin outer shell had protected its liquid interior. But, after sitting through the boiling water, its inside became hardened. The ground coffee beans were unique, however. After they were in the boiling water, they had changed the water and become something better.

"Which are you?" she asked her daughter. *"When trials and adversity knock on your door, how do you respond? Are you a carrot, an egg, or a coffee bean?"*

So which are YOU?

Are you the carrot that seems strong, but with pain and adversity it wilts and becomes soft and loses strength?

Are you the egg that starts with a passive heart and fluid spirit, but changes with the heat? Have you become hardened and stiff from your trials? Does your shell look the same, but, on the inside, you are bitter and tough with a stiff spirit and a hardened heart?

Or, are you like the coffee bean? The bean actually changes the hot water, the very circumstance that brings the pain. When the water gets hot, it releases the fragrance and flavor. If you are like the bean, when things are at their worst, you become better and change the situation around you. When the hour is the darkest and trials are their greatest, do you elevate yourself to another level? How do you handle adversity? Are you a carrot, an egg, or a coffee bean?

May you have enough happiness to make you sweet, enough trials to make you strong, enough sorrow to keep you human, and enough hope to make you happy.

"We deem those happy who from the experience of life have learned to bear its ills without being overcome by them." Juvenal

GROUND RULE #12

Your Cup Runneth Over ~
Count Your Blessings

"When it comes to life, the critical thing is whether you take things for granted or take them with gratitude." G.K. Chesterton

When You Appreciate What You Already Have Your Cup Overflows!

"The more you praise and celebrate your life, the more there is in life to celebrate."
Oprah Winfrey

The ability to practice gratitude is one of life's most valuable lessons. Of all our qualities, gratitude is probably the one that can most change our life, but it's also the one we take most for granted when we get caught up in the ups and downs of life. Many of us think we'll become more grateful when we've got more things to be happy about. But you've got it backwards: *happiness isn't what makes us grateful—gratefulness is what makes us happy.* One of life's true gifts is learning to be happy where we are even when we aren't where we want to be. Real joy begins when we learn to celebrate and cherish what we already have. When we appreciate what we have, our cup overflows with happiness!

Giving thanks is probably the simplest action that can make the most dramatic difference in your life. How regularly you stop to count your blessings will affect how fully you enjoy life. The evidence is in to prove it—studies show that grateful people have more energy and optimism, are better able to bounce back from adversity, are more compassionate and more likely to help others, and are less materialistic and more satisfied with life. And did you know that gratitude is also proven to be good for your physical health? Those who regularly practice gratitude sleep better, catch fewer colds, exercise more, suffer less depression, and gain a general contentment that may counteract stress. Research now shows a daily dose of gratitude not only keeps you happier, but also healthier and better rested!

We have so much to be grateful for, but expressing and living gratitude consistently doesn't come easily to most people. Instead, the vast majority of us spend our days focusing on what's missing from our lives—the things we don't have, the things that would make our life better, or the things our friends have that we wish we also had. The unfortunate reality is that we get what we focus on. When we focus on the things we don't have, we feel like we never have enough. One of our greatest downfalls is the feeling of always thinking we need more, more, more. This is what leaves us unsatisfied and ungrateful. You will never be truly satisfied if you don't first learn to be thankful for what you currently have. You need to realize how rich you are *now*. Grateful living isn't about getting or having more. It's learning to appreciate what you already have. We can all learn a valuable lesson from this famous woman's true story.

Second Cup Story:
You have most likely heard of the famous country music singer-songwriter Dolly Parton. Years ago, she wrote and recorded a song called 'Coat of Many Colors' (which to this day remains Dolly's favorite song she's ever written). Did you know that song represents a very personal story of her childhood? Dolly grew up in a very poor family, so poor in fact, that her mother had to piece together rags to make her a coat one year. The kids at school were very cruel, laughing and making fun of her coat, but she tried to make them understand how special it was to her because of the love her mother had put into every stitch. In fact, Dolly felt that her coat was worth more than all of the other students' clothes and she wore it proudly. She summarizes her feelings very clearly in this last verse of her famous song:
'But they didn't understand it, and I tried to make them see
That one is only poor, only if they choose to be.
Now I know we had no money, but I was rich as I could be
In my coat of many colors, my momma made for me. Made just for me.'

Dolly was so grateful for what she had that she never felt poor. In fact, she felt so rich. You see, gratitude isn't about having the best of everything; it's about making the most of everything you have. Whether we are rich, poor, or somewhere in the middle, we are all blessed. Grateful people aren't necessarily the ones who have the most in their life to be grateful for; they simply learn to focus most on what they currently have. Life is not about possessions, how much you own, or how much you have. It's about learning to be truly thankful for what you've been given.

Fortunately, gratitude is a quality we can learn and improve upon. Anyone can become more grateful. We all have so many things to be grateful for, but without purposeful time to acknowledge them, we don't see the blessings right in front of us. A daily practice of gratitude unlocks a richness of life sweeter than you can imagine. It truly is the key to a happy life. Gratitude changes all that we have from being ordinary into being a gift. It turns what we have into enough and even more! And when this happens, we naturally feel more fulfilled and blessed.

Savoring the true affects of gratitude on your life is much like enjoying a good cup of coffee. If you want it to always taste good, you have to keep warming and refilling it. Fill it once and it tastes great for awhile, but without a warm-up, your cup will soon become cool again. It takes intentional daily effort. Gratitude needs to be brewed into your daily habits. The great news is that you have the power right now to live a life overflowing with gratefulness. Let me give you some ideas of how to make gratitude and appreciation a regular part of your daily life.

"Gratefulness is the key to a happy life that we hold in our hands, because if we are not grateful, then no matter how much we have, we will not be happy because we will always want to have something else or something more." Brother David Steindl-Rast

Grounds for Thought: Do you think your friends and family would characterize you as a grateful person? Why or why not? Do you feel your life is rich or poor? Have you fallen into the 'more, more, more' trap? How regularly do you count your blessings?

JAVA JOLT #1:
Begin Each Day with a Gratitude Coffee Break

"When I first open my eyes upon the morning meadows and look out upon the beautiful world, I thank God I am alive." Ralph Waldo Emerson

When you wake up in the morning and see the glowing sun shining through your window, do you feel gratitude for the gift of another day or do you focus on the multitude of tasks you need to accomplish before the sun slips behind the horizon? It's easy to forget all we have to be thankful for when life becomes hectic and chaotic. There's no doubt that life has become more complicated, but sometimes we need to just stop and reassess our lives and the simple things we have to be grateful for. If you woke up with breath left in you this morning, then you have been blessed. You should give thanks for your life, including the warm bed you're getting out of, being able to put your feet on the floor, to walk to your bathroom, to have a variety of outfits to choose from, to kiss your sleepy children, and to have breakfast to eat. Make a commitment to pause each morning and reflect on your blessings.

One of the easiest ways to become a more grateful person is to begin each day with a gratitude coffee break. Create a gratitude ritual by using your first cup of coffee in the morning as a reminder to take note of the things you feel grateful for. My average morning cup of coffee takes 10 sips to complete. So before I even get my day fully started, I've expressed appreciation for at least 10 things I'm grateful for. Injecting conscious appreciation into your morning routine will help you refocus on what truly matters and will set your mind in the right direction for the rest of the day. Each time you sip your coffee (or whatever beverage you drink to get you going in the morning) reflect on the things you are grateful for. You can start by saying, *"Thank you for another day."* Every time you do this, you are refreshed and refilled.

On any given day, a healthy person should be able to list pages and pages of blessings. But most of us get stuck quickly. We are often blind to all our blessings. Here's a piece of advice: instead of thinking only of those who have more than you, spend time thinking about those who have less. Even on your worst days, you are so much more blessed than many people. If you don't believe me, read the following poem.

**Second Cup Story:** (Author Unknown)

Even though I clutch my blanket and growl when the alarm rings, thank you, Lord, that I can hear. There are many who are deaf.

Even though I keep my eyes closed against the morning light as long as possible, thank you, Lord, that I can see. Many are blind.

Even though I huddle in my bed and put off rising, thank you, Lord, that I have the strength to rise. There are many who are bedridden.

Even though the first hour of my day is hectic, when socks are lost, toast is burned, tempers are short, and my children are so loud, thank you, Lord, for my family. There are many who are lonely.

Even though our breakfast table never looks like the pictures in magazines, and the menu is, at times, unbalanced, thank you, Lord, for the food we have. There are many who are hungry.

Even though the routine of my job often is monotonous, thank you, Lord, for the opportunity to work. There are many who have no job.

Even though I grumble and bemoan my fate from day to day and wish my circumstances were not so modest, thank you, Lord, for life!

"If only the people who worry about their liabilities would think about the riches they do possess, they would stop worrying. Would you sell both your eyes for a million dollars? Or your legs? Or your hands? Or your hearing? Add up what you do have, and you'll find that you won't sell them for all the gold in the world. The best things in life are yours, if you can appreciate yourself." Dale Carnegie

You've been given so many precious gifts: your family, your friends, your sense of humor, the sun, the rain, the ability to see, hear, smell, touch and taste, to be able to eat a good meal, talk on your phone, take aspirin for a headache, or have a bed to make in the morning. Remember even the smallest gestures: being able to hug your child or see your spouse smile at you, being able to smell the toast in the toaster or taste the warmth of coffee on your tongue, having a job to go to or being able to stay home with your children, or enjoying a hot shower with fresh, clean water. If you can learn to appreciate the little things, you'll appreciate the big things and everything in between. You'll find the little things will turn into big things when you fully appreciate them.

Learn to take gratitude coffee breaks and drink in all you are grateful for. Then your morning jolt will offer you a double dose of energy and fulfillment. Making this morning practice a habit will help you to better handle the stresses of the day while making you an all-around happier woman.

Grounds for Thought: What are you most grateful for? Do you have difficulty finding things you appreciate about your life? Are all your basic needs taken care of? How long has it been since you took an inventory of all you have to be grateful for?

Grounds for Action: Start taking gratitude coffee breaks by using your first cup in the morning to celebrate all you have. Take five-ten minutes each morning and focus on everything and everyone you are grateful for. Ask yourself these questions: Who am I thankful for today? Do I have food, clothing, and shelter? Do I have family and friends to count on? Can I hear, see, taste, touch, feel, love, and laugh? Can I enjoy a movie, watch the sunset, listen to a favorite song, eat a favorite food, smell the fresh rain, enjoy the taste of my coffee, hear the birds sing, enjoy the company of pets, and share conversations with loved ones?

Extra Jolt Challenge: Hold a gratitude tea or coffee break with others. Invite friends over for coffee and ask them to bring a list of 10 things they feel grateful for. Throughout the get-together, take turns sharing your lists. You're bound to get more examples of things you can be grateful for, too. Sometimes sharing coffee and conversation with friends is just what we need to get the gratitude flowing.

JAVA JOLT #2:
Remember Your Coffee Etiquette

"God gave you a gift of 86,400 seconds today. Have you used one to say 'thank you?'" William Arthur Ward

You probably heard these words so often growing up: *"Be polite." "Remember to say 'please' and 'thank you.'"* But society these days seems to have forgotten those wise words of advice we get from our parents. Instead, it often seems that appreciation is replaced by a sense of entitlement—a feeling that we are automatically deserving of everything around us. And because of this, appreciation gets thrown out the window. Have you ever been shocked by doing something for someone who never said thank you? Part of learning to be a more grateful person is to remember your coffee etiquette. In other words, mind your manners!

One of the quickest, simplest ways to express gratitude is to say thank you to someone directly. It could be for big things like a gift or help on a project at work, but more often than not, thank you's are for little things—a phone call from a friend, a compliment from a co-worker, or a friendly person holding the door for you. Saying thank you is the simplest way to express gratitude on a daily basis. But if you don't watch yourself, it can easily be overlooked as you rush through your days.

How many times have you rushed through a store and not even stopped to thank the cashier for his or her help while checking out? Don't get too busy to acknowledge those around you. Take time to appreciate the people who help you every day: the worker in the drive-thru, the cashier at the grocery store, the gas attendant, the mailman, the janitor at work, your spouse who makes the coffee in the morning, and your child who picks up his toys. Tell them what a good job they did and how much you appreciated their assistance. Don't make the mistake of assuming people know we are grateful for their services, actions, gifts, or kind acts. Tell them. You might be the first thank you that person has received all day.

"Appreciation can make a day, even change a life. Your willingness to put it into words is all that is necessary." Margaret Cousins

Don't rush so fast through your days concerned only about yourself. Take time to say thank you to the people who help you out every day; make them feel special. Extend appreciation to everyone you meet. When you learn to appreciate those around you, you'll soon find that more people want to be around you. In fact, did you know that waiters and waitresses, on average, get an 11% larger tip when they write thank you on the check? Everyone loves to feel appreciated.

If you long to experience greater joy each day, start saying thank you more often. A simple thank you will positively change your life, and it leaves the others around you feeling good about themselves. Go out of your way to express appreciation and make other people feel good—a loving gesture, a kind word, or a written thank you note. Saying thank you, showing appreciation and making a point of acknowledging others will not only allow your cup to overflow but the person's on the receiving end of that thank you as well. It's true that a simple thank you can affect the way people interact with you.

 Second Cup Story:

I read about a gratitude experiment regarding a group of doctors who were given a bag of candy tied with a note of thanks for their participation in a research project. Another group of doctors was asked to participate in the same research project but was not given any candy or thank you notes. The doctors who were given the bag of candies in this study were better able to process the facts of difficult medical cases and were also more willing to spend extra time evaluating the patient's charts than the physicians who didn't get candy or thank you notes.

Now I'm not saying that candy is what made all the difference (although I'm taking goodies to my next check-up), but think about how this experiment applies in your own life. When someone acknowledges you with small gestures of kindness and appreciation, aren't you more apt to go out of your way to help them? When people feel good and valued, they also feel more positive about the situation. Good feelings are generated by something as simple as an expression of appreciation.

Make a point to say thank you to someone today. As you begin making it more of a habit, start challenging yourself to say thanks to more and more people each day. See how many people you can thank in a day: the mailman, the soda delivery man at work, a great friend for calling, a parent for offering encouragement, a spouse for making you laugh, a restaurant worker for the great service, a boss for his or her mentoring, the hygienist at the dentist office, the office worker who makes the morning coffee, the newspaper delivery person… Get the point? It really isn't hard; it just sometimes takes a little reminding much like our parents used to do for us years ago. Hey, that reminds me, Thanks, Mom!

Grounds for Thought: Have you ever helped someone who never said thank you? Ever given a gift and never received proper thanks? How many people do you thank in an average day?

Grounds for Action: Remember your manners. Say thank you to everyone who helps you today. Perhaps, you can even remember someone with a small gift of appreciation. Make a point to appreciate as many people as possible every day.

JAVA JOLT #3:
Refresh the Day's Blessings At Bedtime

"Before you go to bed, thank God for everyone and everything. Count your blessings; name them one by one." Dr. Norman Vincent Peale

In the evening, when most of us review our day, we usually focus on everything that went wrong or that was irritating to us—a rude customer, a disrespectful co-worker, a dirty house, an empty gas tank, a low balance in the check book, or a misbehaving child. Sound familiar? Many things happen every day that you are thankful for, but you don't usually pay attention to them. They get drowned out by the bad. Appreciating all the goodness around you includes learning to count your blessings again at bedtime. Giving thanks before bedtime can be a delightful ritual that helps develop a healthy and grateful attitude toward life.

Recording your blessings before going to sleep has actually been proven to improve sleep habits. Interestingly, it's not enough to simply say what you are grateful for. You must write it down according to researchers. Those who merely think about their blessings don't feel the same level of happiness as those who write them down. Apparently, there is power in the written word. Plus, it's fun to look back and see all of the ways you've been blessed. So rather than counting sheep to cure insomnia, try counting your blessings!

To start your evening gratitude habit, keep a notebook or journal at your bedside. Before you go to bed, reflect on these statements: *Today I am grateful for…* or *Three great things about today were…* Some days may feel like nothing went right and that makes it even more important to dig deeply to find something to be grateful for. I've made it a daily habit to spend three to five minutes in the evening before going to bed writing down a few things I am thankful for that day. I can't help but smile when my head hits the pillow. And it makes a bad day seem not quite so discouraging. Then, in the morning, I wake with my cherished routine of reviewing my list over my morning coffee. It's a great way to start and end the day.

As you review your day, remember even the smallest gestures. Here's a few ideas I took from my journal: encouragement from a friend, free samples at the grocery store, a good hair day, a hug from my mom, getting my freshly washed jeans on and zipped, enjoying freshly popped microwave kettle corn, homemade soup from my aunt, a note I received in the mail, watching my cat sleep, my favorite slipper socks, finding a $5 bill in my pants pocket, the cozy fire in my fireplace, clean sheets on my bed, the smell of my favorite candle, my favorite song on the radio when the alarm went off, a delicious piece of carrot cake with my coffee, my new silver and pink tennis shoes…

Research shows the more you work on developing your gratitude bone, the more your life will come alive. When you practice an evening gratitude ritual, you naturally search for kindness, love, and goodness throughout the day so that you'll have something new in mind to be grateful for when bedtime rolls around. It takes your mind off the irritating elements of your day and places your focus on the good things. Don't just give thanks during your morning gratitude coffee break. Make it a nightly habit that every evening before bed you'll take time to count your blessings before your head hits the pillow.

Grounds for Thought: Do you ever find yourself having difficulty sleeping because you're replaying all the bad things from the day? Do you even remember the good things about your day? How often do you count your blessings at bedtime?

Grounds for Action: Grab a small notebook to place by your bed. Start making a note of three things you are grateful for at the end of each day. What new opportunities are you thankful for? What challenges did you overcome that you are thankful for? Who helped you today that you're grateful for? Who were you able to help today?

The Last Cup

"The hardest arithmetic to master is that which enables us to count our blessings."
Eric Hoffer

Whether you realize it or not, you *are* richly blessed. There is plenty in your life to be thankful for as long as you purposely look for it. Whether you like your life or not doesn't depend on how much you have; it's how much you appreciate what you have. Appreciation is a matter of perspective. You can train yourself to be a more grateful person.

People who focus on living with an attitude of gratitude as part of their daily routine are happier people. They see their lives more favorably and have less health issues. Life just seems to be better for those who focus on what they are grateful for versus those who focus on what they are lacking or would like to change.

One of the greatest joys in our lives comes from discovering and practicing daily gratitude. Understanding that you should be grateful won't help much if you don't put it into practice. Make a commitment to pause each day and reflect on your blessings and appreciate more of the people around you with a simple expression of thank you. By nurturing your ability to express gratitude you will begin to have a greater appreciation for your life.

Beginning and ending each day with gratitude is a good thing to do. When we begin filling our cups with a daily inventory of the things we most appreciate, happiness and contentment start to flow. Take time to count your blessings; you'll soon realize your cup runneth over!

"Joy is what happens when we allow ourselves to recognize how good things really are."
Marianne Williamson

Break's Over...You Better Get to Living!

"The best inheritance you can leave your kids is an example of how to live a full and meaningful life." Dan Zadra

I want to thoroughly express my gratitude for taking the time to join me for Inspirational Coffee Breaks. I hope these 12 Ground Rules excite and challenge you to live each day more fully. Within you lies the promise of a fresh-brewed future. My wish for you is that Inspirational Coffee Breaks will become a life-long ritual to help you keep growing, learning, and getting better. And that with every sip, you get even closer to becoming the woman you want to be.

So until we meet again...

May your cup runneth over, and your special blend may you find,
And may you take enough chances to burn your tongue time to time.
May you remember who's in control of your personal brew,
For your life's attitude and goals are determined by you.
May the cracks in your cup be something you treasure,
And others' cups that you fill be far beyond measure.
May you also leave room for cream and sugar, indeed,
For love, laughter, and rest are all things we need.
And may The Inspirational Coffee Club inspire you to savor today,
By living life to the fullest and brewing it your way.

Live life like COFFEE!
Let's tip our cups to life and for many more Inspirational Coffee Breaks together!

Julie

Julie Clark, Founder
The Inspirational Coffee Club

About the Author

Julie Clark is a speaker, author, and founder of The Inspirational Coffee Club, sharing creative messages, strategies, and stories that teach women how to pour their hearts into a life that overflows with fulfillment. Julie knew from an early age that coffee was far more than just a drink to her. At three-years old, she started drinking coffee and dunking cookies with her Norwegian Grandma, and since then, she has never missed a day without coffee. Over the years, coffee has become a metaphor for how Julie lives life. She has developed a unique blend of strategies called '12 Ground Rules for Life' to help women live life to the fullest.

Julie has developed an innovative approach to applying these Ground Rules—a method she calls Inspirational Coffee Breaks. Her first book, *Inspirational Coffee Breaks for Women* is revolutionizing the way women take their coffee breaks, teaching others how to transform ordinary coffee breaks into recipes for success, happiness, and joy.

Julie's messages provide just the right blend of fun, inspiration and motivation to give your life a boost. Her Inspirational Coffee Club supports you in becoming the woman you've always wanted to become, encourages you to create a future brimming with enjoyment, and challenges you to savor each day more fully.

A popular speaker at women's events, meetings, expos, and conferences, Julie's inspirational presentations leave audiences with a fresh perspective and renewed enthusiasm for life. Through her speaking, personal coaching, workshops, and products, Julie is helping women of all ages pour their hearts into life.

Visit www.theinspirationalcoffeeclub.com to become an official member of the FREE Inspirational Coffee Club.

the inspirational
coffee club.

PO Box 87922
Sioux Falls, SD 57109
www.theinspirationalcoffeeclub.com
Julie@theinspirationalcoffeeclub.com